UNLOCKING EFFICIENCY

Tally Techniques for Small Business Accounting

UMA DEVI M

ISBN 979-8-89556-397-7

Table of Contents

Introduction..*13*

Acknowledgement *15*

Foreword...*17*

Chapter 1: Introduction to Tally for Small Businesses **19**

   1.1   Why Tally? 19

        Simplicity and Ease of Use: 20

        Comprehensive Functionality: 20

        Customization and Scalability: 20

        Real-Time Financial Insights: 21

        Compliance and Accuracy: 21

        Support and Community: 21

   1.2   Getting Started with Tally 22

        Installing Tally 22

        Setting Up Your Company in Tally 24

        Activating and Licensing Tally 24

        Navigating the Tally Interface 25

        Customizing Tally for Your Business 26

        Getting Help and Support 26

   1.3   Understanding Core Concepts 27

        Introduction to Accounting Principles 27

        Chart of Accounts 27

        Accounting Vouchers 28

        Inventory Management 29

Taxation and Compliance 29

Reporting and Analysis 30

Conclusion 30

Chapter 2: Mastering Tally's Core Features 32

2.1   Creating and Configuring Company Profiles.... 33

Introduction 33

Creating a New Company 33

Configuring Company Settings 34

Managing Multiple Companies 34

Backing Up and Restoring Company Data 36

2.2   Managing Ledgers and Groups 37

Introduction to Ledgers and Groups 37

Creating Ledgers 37

Creating Groups 38

Altering and Deleting Ledgers and Groups 39

Hierarchical Structure and Grouping 39

Practical Examples and Best Practices 39

2.3   Processing Transactions 40

Introduction to Transactions 40

Recording Transactions 41

Managing Recurring Transactions 41

Adjusting Entries 42

Bank Reconciliation 42

Handling Errors 42

Generating Transaction Reports 43

Conclusion 43

Chapter 3: Automating Accounting Tasks 44

3.1   Utilizing Automation Features 45

1. Introduction to Automation in Tally 45

2. Automating Data Entry 45

3. Automating Financial Reports 45

4. Streamlining Transactions with
   Automation 46

5. Managing Inventory with Automation 46

6. Automating Compliance and
   Tax Reporting 47

7. Practical Exercise 47

3.2 Customizing Automation................................. 47

1. Introduction to Customizing Automation 48

2. Customizing Automated Data Entry............ 48

3. Tailoring Financial Reports Automation....... 49

4. Personalizing Transaction Automation 49

5. Customizing Inventory Automation 50

6. Adapting Compliance and
   Tax Automation 51

7. Practical Exercise 51

3.3 Practical Exercises for Automation 52

1. Introduction to Practical Exercises................ 52

2. Setting Up Automated Data Entry............... 53

3. Automating Financial Reports 53

4. Personalizing Transaction Automation 54

5. Customizing Inventory Automation 55

6. Adapting Compliance and
   Tax Automation 56

7. Reviewing and Testing Customizations 57

8. Conclusion 57

Chapter 4: Financial Reporting and Analysis.............59

4.1 Generating Financial Reports 60

1. Introduction to Financial Reports................. 60

2. Types of Financial Reports in Tally 60

3. Generating Reports in Tally 61

4. Customizing Reports 62

5. Reviewing and Analyzing Reports 63

6. Practical Exercise 63

4.2   Analyzing Financial Data 64

1. Introduction to Financial Data Analysis 64

2. Key Financial Metrics and Ratios 65

3. Analyzing Financial Reports 66

4. Comparative and Trend Analysis 67

5. Interpreting Financial Data 68

6. Practical Exercise 68

7. Conclusion 69

4.3   Using Reports for Decision Making 69

1. Introduction to Decision-Making
Using Financial Reports 70

2. Analyzing Financial Reports for
Strategic Decisions 70

3. Using Reports to Drive Operational
Improvements 71

4. Strategic Planning and Forecasting 72

5. Decision-Making Scenarios 72

6. Communicating Financial Insights 73

7. Practical Exercise 73

8. Conclusion 74

Chapter 5: Managing Inventory and Stock 76

5.1   Setting Up Inventory 77

1. Configuring Inventory Settings: 77

2. Creating Stock Items: 77

3. Setting Up Units of Measurement: 78

4. Stock Valuation Methods:................................ 78

5. Managing Stock Transfers:............................. 78

6. Regular Review and Updates: 79

5.2 Tracking Stock Movements............................... 79

1. Recording Purchases: 80

2. Managing Sales Transactions: 80

3. Tracking Stock Adjustments: 80

4. Managing Stock Transfers:............................. 81

5. Utilizing Inventory Reports: 81

6. Conducting Regular Stock Audits: 82

7. Best Practices for Accurate Tracking:............ 82

5.3 Generating Inventory Reports 82

1. Accessing Inventory Reports in Tally:........... 83

2. Generating Stock Summary Reports: 83

3. Analyzing Stock Item Movements:............... 83

4. Utilizing Stock Journal Reports: 84

5. Generating Valuation Reports:...................... 84

6. Customizing Reports for Business

Needs: 84

7. Exporting and Sharing Reports: 85

8. Best Practices for Reporting:......................... 85

Chapter 6: Payroll Management................................**87**

6.1 Configuring Payroll Settings 88

1. Activating Payroll Features:........................... 88

2. Creating Payroll Masters:............................... 88

3. Configuring Salary Components: 89

4. Setting Up Statutory Deductions:................. 89

5. Establishing Payroll Periods:......................... 89

6. Configuring Payroll Reports: 90

7. Review and Testing: 90

6.2   Processing Payroll...................................... 91
        1. Preparing Payroll Data: 91
        2. Generating Payroll Vouchers:........................ 91
        3. Calculating Salaries:..................................... 92
        4. Processing Statutory Deductions: 92
        5. Generating Pay Slips:.................................... 92
        6. Processing Payments: 93
        7. Generating Payroll Reports:.......................... 93
        8. Compliance and Record-Keeping: 93
        9. Finalizing Payroll: 94

6.3   Payroll Reports and Compliance...................... 94
        1. Generating Payroll Reports:.......................... 94
        2. Analyzing Payroll Reports:............................ 95
        3. Ensuring Compliance: 96
        4. Handling Statutory Compliance:................... 96
        5. Audits and Reconciliation:............................ 97
        6. Reviewing and Updating Payroll
           Processes:.. 97

Chapter 7: Taxation and Compliance 98

7.1   Setting Up Taxation 99
        Overview of Taxation in Tally........................... 99
        Step-by-Step Guide to Setting Up Taxation 99
        Practical Example: Setting Up GST for a
        Product Sale... 102
        Tips for Efficient Taxation Management 103

7.2   Calculating and Reporting Taxes 103
        Overview of Tax Calculation in Tally 103
        Step-by-Step Guide to Calculating Taxes 104
        Step-by-Step Guide to Reporting Taxes......... 105

Practical Example: Generating a
GSTR-3B Report.. 107
Tips for Efficient Tax Calculation and
Reporting... 108

7.3   Ensuring Compliance 108
Overview of Compliance in Tally 109
Step-by-Step Guide to Ensuring
Compliance.. 109
Practical Example: Conducting a GST
Reconciliation 112
Tips for Ensuring Compliance 113
Conclusion... 113

Chapter 8: Troubleshooting and Best Practices 114

8.1   Common Issues and Solutions......................... 115

8.2   Best Practices for Accounting 120

8.3   Resources and Support................................... 124
Official Tally Resources 125
External Support and Community 127
Technical Support.. 128
Conclusion... 129

Chapter 9: Case Studies and Success Stories............. 130

9.1   Success Stories from Tally Users 131
Case Study 1: Streamlining Small
Business Accounting....................................... 131
Case Study 2: Enhancing Financial
Management for a Growing Enterprise.......... 132
Case Study 3: Transforming Accounting
Practices in a Non-Profit Organization 133

Lessons Learned from the above
case studies... 133

9.2 Lessons Learned 134
Lesson 1: Proper Implementation is
Crucial 134
Lesson 2: Training and Support
Are Essential... 135
Lesson 3: Utilizing Tally's Features
Effectively.. 136
Lesson 4: Data Accuracy and Security............ 137
Lesson 5: Continuous Improvement
and Adaptation 137

9.3 Applying Insights to Your Business.................. 138
1. Assessing Your Current Accounting
Practices 139
2. Customizing Tally to Meet Your Needs...... 139
3. Training and Engaging Your Team 140
4. Ensuring Data Accuracy and Security 141
5. Monitoring and Adapting to Changes........ 142
Conclusion.. 142

Chapter 10: Conclusion and Next Steps 144

10.1 Recap of Key Learnings 145
1. Understanding Tally's Core Features........... 145
2. Importance of Proper Implementation 146
3. Training and Support for Effective Use 146
4. Ensuring Data Accuracy and Security 146
5. Adapting to Changes and Continuous
Improvement... 147

10.2 Planning for Future Growth 148
1. Assessing Growth Potential........................ 148

2. Scaling Your Tally Implementation 149

3. Optimizing Processes for Efficiency 149

4. Training and Development for a
   Growing Team 150

5. Planning for Technological
   Advancements 151

6. Building a Long-Term Strategy 152

10.3 Continuing Your Education 153

1. The Importance of Ongoing Learning 153

2. Educational Resources and
   Opportunities 154

3. Setting Personal and Professional
   Learning Goals 155

4. Applying New Knowledge and Skills 156

5. Staying Engaged with Professional
   Communities 156

Conclusion 157

Introduction

In today's fast-paced business environment, efficiency is not just an advantage but a necessity. For small businesses, effective management of finances and accounting can significantly impact overall performance and growth. With the right tools and techniques, even complex accounting processes can become streamlined and manageable. This is where Tally, one of the most widely used accounting software, plays a crucial role.

Welcome to *Unlocking Efficiency: Tally Techniques for Small Business Accounting.* This book is crafted to be a comprehensive guide for small business owners, accountants, and anyone looking to leverage the power of Tally to enhance their accounting practices. Whether you are a novice or have some experience with Tally, this book aims to provide valuable insights and practical techniques to help you unlock the full potential of the software.

The journey through this book will begin with a foundational understanding of Tally, covering essential aspects such as installation, company creation, and basic settings. We will then delve into mastering Tally's core features, including accounting, inventory management, and report generation. Each chapter is designed to build your knowledge progressively, ensuring that you gain a thorough understanding of how to use Tally effectively.

One of the key highlights of this book is the focus on real-world applications. We will explore success stories from various Tally users who have successfully implemented these techniques in their businesses. These stories will provide practical examples of how Tally can be used to address common challenges and drive efficiency.

Furthermore, this book emphasizes the importance of continuous improvement and learning. As technology and business practices evolve, so too must our approach to accounting. The final sections of the book will guide you on how to plan for future growth, continue your education, and stay updated with new developments in Tally and accounting practices.

Unlocking Efficiency is more than just a technical manual; it is a resource designed to empower you with the knowledge and skills needed to transform your accounting processes. By applying the techniques and insights shared in this book, you will be well-equipped to enhance your financial management practices and contribute to the success of your business.

Thank you for choosing this book as your guide. I hope you find the information and techniques shared here to be valuable and transformative. Let's embark on this journey towards greater efficiency and excellence in accounting with Tally.

Acknowledgement

I am deeply grateful to everyone who has contributed to the creation of this book, ***Unlocking Efficiency: Tally Techniques for Small Business Accounting.*** This journey has been a collaborative effort, and I am thankful for the support and encouragement I've received along the way.

Firstly, I want to extend my heartfelt gratitude to my Parents & my husband, whose unwavering support and insightful advice have been my guiding light throughout this project. His belief in my vision and his continuous encouragement have been invaluable. I would also like to express my gratitude to the Diamond Membership community & Dr. Manjunath.

I am also profoundly appreciative of my colleagues and peers in the accounting field, whose practical insights and experiences have greatly enriched the content of this book. Your shared knowledge has been instrumental in shaping the practical tips and success stories that are featured here.

A special thanks to the Tally team for providing such a robust platform that has made it possible to streamline accounting processes and enhance efficiency. Your dedication to innovation and user support has been a source of inspiration.

Finally, I want to acknowledge all the readers and users of Tally who have shared their success stories and experiences. Your real-world applications and feedback have helped to shape this book into a practical guide aimed at unlocking efficiency for small business accounting.

Thank you all for being a part of this journey and for helping make *Unlocking Efficiency* a reality.

With Gratitude
Uma Devi M

Foreword

In the ever-evolving world of accounting, staying ahead of the curve requires not only knowledge but also the ability to harness technology effectively. Tally, as a powerful tool, has become indispensable for businesses seeking to streamline their financial operations. However, few professionals are able to truly unlock the full potential of this software and integrate it seamlessly into everyday business practices.

In *"Unlocking Efficiency - Tally Techniques for Small Business Accounting,"* Uma Devi has crafted an insightful and practical guide that fills this gap, especially for small business owners and accountants looking to enhance their efficiency. With over 9 years of experience as an Accounts Manager, Uma brings invaluable hands-on knowledge and an expert perspective on how to best utilize Tally for real-world applications.

This book goes beyond basic Tally functions, providing readers with tips, techniques, and strategies that are critical for maximizing productivity, ensuring accuracy, and ultimately making more informed financial decisions. It is designed to help users at every skill level—whether you are just starting out or looking to optimize your workflows—to benefit from the features that Tally offers.

In today's competitive business environment, gaining mastery over such tools can make all the difference. I am confident that this book will become an essential resource for anyone who wants to sharpen their accounting skills while managing the financial intricacies of small businesses. I wholeheartedly recommend this guide for its clarity, depth, and practical insights.

Wishing you success in your journey towards mastering Tally and unlocking its potential for your business.

– Dr CA Ravi Agarwal
Founder of CA Mentoring Program in India

CHAPTER 1

Introduction to Tally for Small Businesses

This chapter introduces small business owners to Tally, a powerful accounting software designed to simplify financial management. You'll learn the basics of Tally, including its key features and benefits tailored to small businesses. The chapter covers how Tally can streamline accounting tasks, improve accuracy, and enhance financial reporting. By the end, you'll understand how Tally can be leveraged to efficiently manage your business finances, from setting up your company profile to navigating the core functionalities.

1.1 Why Tally?

In this section, we delve into the compelling reasons why Tally is a highly recommended accounting software for small businesses. Understanding these benefits will help you appreciate the value Tally brings to your business operations and financial management.

Simplicity and Ease of Use:

Tally is renowned for its user-friendly interface and straightforward design. Unlike many complex accounting systems, Tally offers an intuitive experience that simplifies tasks for users, whether they are seasoned accountants or novices. This ease of use ensures that you can quickly adapt to the software, minimizing the learning curve and enabling you to focus more on running your business.

Comprehensive Functionality:

Tally provides a wide range of features that cover all aspects of small business accounting. From managing day-to-day transactions, such as sales and purchases, to handling complex functions like inventory management, payroll, and tax calculations, Tally integrates these functionalities into one seamless platform. This comprehensive approach reduces the need for multiple software solutions and ensures that all your financial data is centralized and easily accessible.

Customization and Scalability:

One of Tally's strengths is its flexibility. It can be tailored to meet the specific needs of various types of businesses, whether you run a retail store, a manufacturing unit, or a service-based enterprise. Additionally, Tally's scalability allows it to grow with your business. As your business expands, you can easily adjust the software to accommodate increased transactions, additional users, and more complex accounting requirements.

Real-Time Financial Insights:

Tally's real-time reporting capabilities provide you with up-to-date financial information at your fingertips. This feature is crucial for making informed business decisions, monitoring cash flow, and analyzing financial performance. With Tally, you can generate detailed reports such as balance sheets and profit & loss statements, which help you understand your financial position and plan strategically.

Compliance and Accuracy:

Maintaining compliance with accounting standards and tax regulations is essential for any business. Tally helps you stay compliant by offering built-in features for accurate tax calculations, statutory compliance, and reporting. This reduces the risk of errors and ensures that your financial practices align with regulatory requirements.

Support and Community:

Tally benefits from a robust support network and a vibrant user community. Whether you need technical assistance, have questions about features, or want to share experiences with other users, you can access a wealth of resources. Tally's official support channels, online forums, and user groups provide valuable guidance and help ensure that you get the most out of the software.

In summary, Tally stands out as a versatile and user-friendly accounting solution that offers extensive features, customization options, and real-time insights. Its ability to streamline financial management and adapt to growing business needs makes it a valuable tool for small businesses aiming to enhance their accounting practices and drive success.

1.2   Getting Started with Tally

Overview:

- Tally is a robust accounting software designed to streamline business operations. Understanding its core features and historical evolution helps appreciate its value in modern business.

Key Features:

- Comprehensive accounting solutions
- Inventory management
- Taxation and compliance (GST, VAT, etc.)
- Payroll management
- Multi-language support

Installing Tally

System Requirements:

- **Hardware:** Minimum dual-core processor, 1 GB RAM (2 GB recommended), 512 MB free disk space.
- **Software:** Windows 7 or higher, Microsoft Office for report export.

Downloading Tally:

- Visit the official Tally Solutions website to download the latest version.

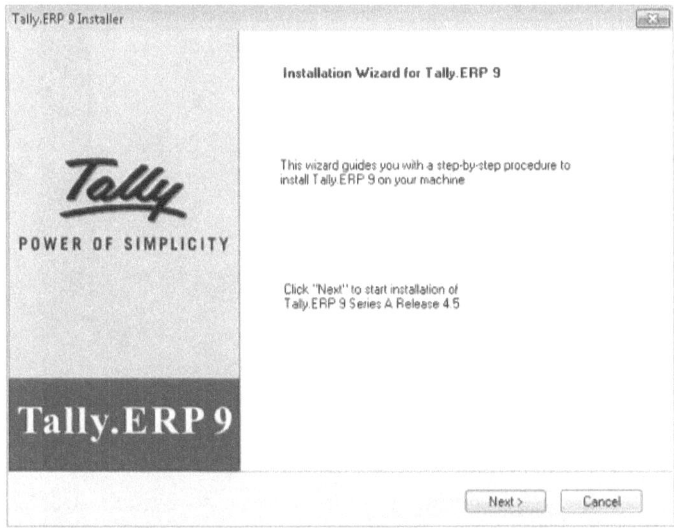

Installation Process:

- **Step 1:** Run the downloaded installer.
- **Step 2:** Follow the installation wizard.
- **Step 3:** Choose installation destination.
- **Step 4:** Complete the installation by following on-screen instructions.

Troubleshooting:

- Common installation errors and solutions.
- Contact Tally support for unresolved issues.

Setting Up Your Company in Tally

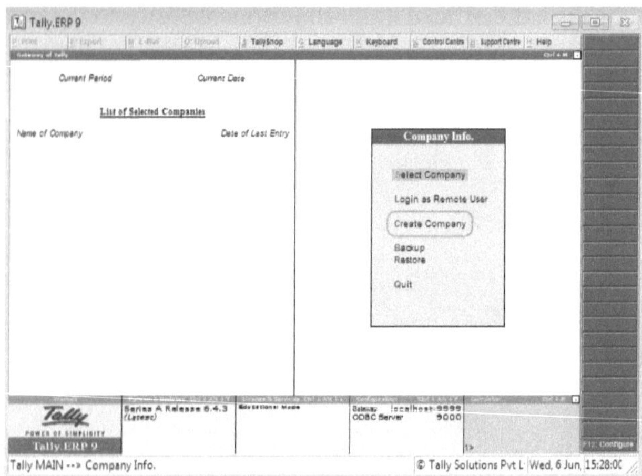

Creating a New Company:

- Go to "Create Company" from the Tally home screen.
- Enter essential details: company name, address, financial year, currency, etc.

Configuration Settings:

- Set up base currency, taxation details, and other preferences.

Activating and Licensing Tally

License Types:

- Single-user and multi-user licenses.

Activation Process:

- Enter the activation key provided upon purchase.
- Follow prompts for online activation.

License Renewal and Upgrades:

Instructions for renewing licenses or upgrading to a newer version.

- **Step 1:** Open Tally
- **Step 2:** Access the Licensing Menu
- **Step 3:** Renew License
- **Step 4:** Enter License Information
- **Step 5:** Make Payment
- **Step 6:** License Renewal Confirmation
- **Step 7:** Restart Tally

Navigating the Tally Interface

Home Screen Layout:

- Gateway of Tally: central hub for accessing all features.
- Menu Bar: top navigation for primary functions.
- Button Bar: right-side shortcuts for frequent tasks.
- Info Panel: bottom section displaying company details and date.

Menus and Options:

Detailed explanation of main menus and their functions.

- **F1:** Select Company
- **F2:** Change Period
- **F3:** Company Info
- **F4 to F10:** Quick Navigation for Vouchers
- **F11:** Features
- **F12:** Configuration

Customizing Tally for Your Business

User Preferences:

- Adjust appearance and layout.
- Set up user roles and permissions.

Configuration Options:

- Advanced settings for specialized business needs.
- Customizing reports and data entry forms.

Getting Help and Support

In-Built Help:

- Utilize Tally's built-in help features and tutorials.
- Access the Tally Knowledge Base for self-help resources.

Customer Support:

- Contact Tally support for technical assistance.
- Use community forums and online resources for additional help.

Summary:

- Recap of steps to get started with Tally.
- Emphasis on the importance of proper setup for efficient accounting.

Next Steps:

- Preparing for deeper exploration of Tally's features in subsequent chapters.

This section ensures that you have a solid foundation for using Tally effectively, covering everything from installation to initial setup and basic navigation, paving the way for more advanced functionalities.

1.3   Understanding Core Concepts

Introduction to Accounting Principles

Basic Accounting Principles:

- **Double-Entry System:** Understanding debits and credits, and the concept of balancing accounts.
- **Accrual Basis vs. Cash Basis:** Key differences and implications for financial reporting.
- **Fundamental Accounting Equation:** Assets = Liabilities + Equity.

Chart of Accounts

Definition and Importance:

- The **Chart of Accounts (COA)** is an essential component of any accounting system, serving as the organizational blueprint for a company's financial records. It is a complete listing of all accounts that a business uses to record its financial transactions, structured in a logical and systematic manner
- Organizing accounts into assets, liabilities, income, expenses, and equity.

Creating a Chart of Accounts:

Steps to set up a chart of accounts in Tally.

- Gateway of Tally > Chart of Accounts > Ledgers and press Enter.

Categorizing accounts for better financial management.

- Assets
- Liabilities
- Income
- Expenditure

Accounting Vouchers

Types of Vouchers:

- **Payment Vouchers:** Recording outgoing payments.
- **Receipt Vouchers:** Documenting incoming receipts.
- **Sales Vouchers:** Capturing sales transactions.
- **Purchase Vouchers:** Recording purchases.
- **Journal Vouchers:** General adjustments and transfers.
- **Contra Voucher:** involving cash and bank accounts

Entering Vouchers in Tally:

Step-by-step guide to entering different types of vouchers.

1. Navigate to Payment Voucher:

Go to Gateway of Tally > Accounting Vouchers > Select F5: Payment.

2. Navigate to Receipt Voucher:

Go to Gateway of Tally > Accounting Vouchers > Select F6: Receipt.

3. Navigate to Sales Voucher:

Go to Gateway of Tally > Accounting Vouchers > Select F8: Sales.

4. Navigate to Purchase Voucher:

Go to Gateway of Tally > Accounting Vouchers > Select F9: Purchase.

5. Navigate to Journal Voucher:

Go to Gateway of Tally > Accounting Vouchers > Select F7: Journal.

6. Navigate to Contra Voucher:

Go to Gateway of Tally > Accounting Vouchers > Select F4: Contra.

Inventory Management

Inventory Basics:

- Understanding stock items, stock groups, and units of measure.
- Importance of accurate inventory tracking for business success.

Managing Inventory in Tally:

- Creating and maintaining stock items.
- Recording inventory transactions and adjustments.

Taxation and Compliance

Tax Basics:

- Overview of common business taxes (e.g., GST, VAT, income tax).
- Importance of compliance with tax regulations.

Tally's Taxation Features:

- Setting up tax rates and categories in Tally.
- Recording tax-related transactions and generating reports.

Reporting and Analysis

Financial Reports:

- Key financial reports: Balance Sheet, Profit & Loss Statement, Cash Flow Statement.
- How to generate and interpret these reports in Tally.

Analytical Tools:

- Utilizing Tally's built-in tools for financial analysis.
- Customizing reports to meet specific business needs.

Conclusion

Summary:

- Recap of core accounting concepts and their application in Tally.
- Emphasis on the importance of understanding these concepts for effective financial management.

Next Steps:

- Encouragement to apply these concepts in daily accounting tasks.
- Preparing for more advanced topics in subsequent chapters.

This chapter aims to provide a solid foundation in essential accounting concepts and demonstrate how Tally facilitates efficient financial management through practical application.

"Mastering Tally is more than learning software; it's about gaining control over your business's financial pulse, transforming numbers into insights that drive growth."

CHAPTER 2

Mastering Tally's Core Features

This chapter delves into the essential features of Tally that streamline accounting and business management. You'll explore:

- **Ledger Management:** Creating, organizing, and maintaining financial accounts.
- **Voucher Entry:** Efficiently recording various financial transactions.
- **Inventory Control:** Tracking and managing stock items and inventory.
- **Financial Reporting:** Generating and interpreting key financial reports.
- **Tax Compliance:** Setting up and managing tax details, ensuring compliance with regulations.

- **Advanced Features:** Customizing Tally to fit specific business needs and enhance productivity.

By mastering these core features, you'll enhance your proficiency in using Tally for effective and accurate business management.

2.1 Creating and Configuring Company Profiles

Introduction

Importance of Company Profiles:

- Understanding why setting up a company profile is essential for accurate financial management and reporting in Tally.

Creating a New Company

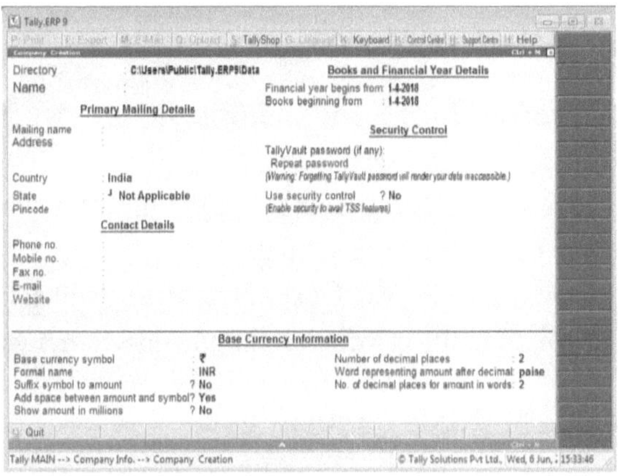

Steps to Create a Company:

- **Step 1:** Navigate to the "Create Company" option in Tally.

- **Step 2:** Fill in essential details like company name, address, financial year start date, and base currency.
- **Step 3:** Save the company profile.

Key Fields Explained:

- Explanation of critical fields during company creation, including legal name, mailing name, and financial year details.

Configuring Company Settings

Initial Configuration:

- **Base Currency:** Set the base currency and format.
- **Financial Year:** Configure the financial year and book beginning dates.
- **Security Controls:** Set up user roles and passwords for secure access.

Advanced Configuration:

- **Taxation:** Enable and configure tax settings such as GST, VAT, and service tax.
- **Inventory Management:** Enable inventory features and configure stock settings.
- **Custom Features:** Customize settings like invoice formats, multi-currency, and multi-location inventory.

Managing Multiple Companies

Creating Additional Companies:

- Steps to create and configure additional companies within Tally.

- o   Open Tally.
- o   Select "Create Company".
- o   Fill in the company details (Name, Address, Financial Year, etc.).
- o   Press Ctrl + A to save

Switching Between Companies:

- How to seamlessly switch between multiple companies for efficient management.

  - o   Load Companies: Press F1 (Select Company), choose multiple companies using the Spacebar, and press Enter.
  - o   Switch Companies: Press Alt + F3, select "Select Company", and choose the company to work on.
  - o   Quick Toggle: Use Alt + F1 to switch between open companies.

Consolidating Financial Data:

- Techniques for consolidating financial data across multiple companies for comprehensive reporting.

  - o   Load Companies: Press F1 (Select Company) and load all companies.
  - o   Enable Group Company: Press Alt + F3 > Create Group Company. Select the companies to include.
  - o   View Consolidated Reports: Access reports like Trial Balance, Profit & Loss, or Balance Sheet for the group.

Backing Up and Restoring Company Data

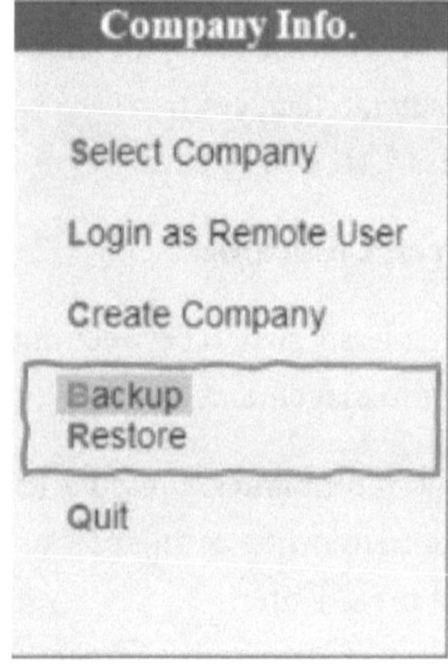

Backup Process:

Steps to regularly back up company data to prevent data loss.

- Go to **Gateway of Tally > F3: Cmp Info > Backup**.

Restoration Process:

Instructions for restoring company data from backups in case of data loss or corruption.

- **Go to** Gateway of Tally > **F3**: Cmp Info > Restore.

Summary:

- Recap of the importance and process of creating and configuring company profiles.

Next Steps:

- Preparing to dive into more detailed aspects of Tally's core features in subsequent chapters.

This section ensures that users have a solid foundation in setting up and managing company profiles in Tally, crucial for accurate and efficient financial management.

2.2   Managing Ledgers and Groups

Introduction to Ledgers and Groups

Understanding Ledgers: Ledgers are the individual accounts where financial transactions are recorded. They serve as the building blocks of your accounting system, capturing detailed information about various aspects of your business, such as sales, purchases, cash, and bank transactions.

Understanding Groups: Groups categorize ledgers into meaningful segments, making it easier to manage and report financial data. Common groups include Sundry Debtors, Sundry Creditors, and Capital Account, each serving a specific role in organizing your financial information.

Creating Ledgers

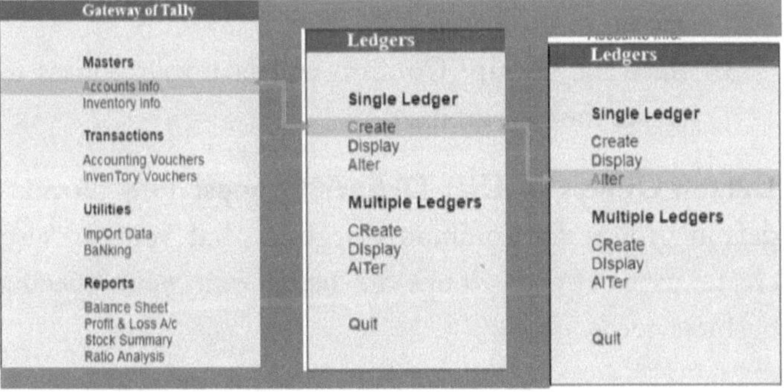

Steps to Create a Ledger:

1. **Navigate to Creation:** Go to "Gateway of Tally" > "Accounts Info" > "Ledgers" > "Create."
2. **Enter Details:** Fill in the ledger name, select the appropriate group, and complete other necessary fields such as the opening balance.
3. **Save the Ledger:** Confirm and save your entries to create the new ledger.

Key Fields Explained:

- **Name:** The name of the ledger account.
- **Under Group:** The category to which the ledger belongs.
- **Opening Balance:** The initial balance of the ledger.

Creating Groups

Steps to Create a Group:

1. **Navigate to Creation:** Go to "Gateway of Tally" > "Accounts Info" > "Groups" > "Create."
2. **Enter Details:** Provide the group name, specify whether it is a primary or sub-group, and other relevant information.
3. **Save the Group:** Confirm and save your entries to create the new group.

Default Groups vs. User-Defined Groups: Tally provides default groups for common categories, but you can also create user-defined groups to better suit your specific business needs.

Altering and Deleting Ledgers and Groups

Altering Ledgers: Modify existing ledgers by navigating to "Alter" in the ledgers menu, making necessary changes, and saving the updated ledger.

Altering Groups: Similarly, modify existing groups by navigating to "Alter" in the groups menu, updating details, and saving the changes.

Deleting Ledgers and Groups: Delete unwanted ledgers and groups carefully by selecting them in the alter menu and using the delete option, ensuring that no dependencies are overlooked.

Hierarchical Structure and Grouping

Group Hierarchy: Understand the hierarchical structure of groups in Tally, where primary groups can have sub-groups, allowing for detailed categorization.

Benefits of Grouping: Grouping ledgers into appropriate categories simplifies reporting and analysis, enhancing data organization and management efficiency.

Practical Examples and Best Practices

Examples: Illustrative case studies showing how to create and manage ledgers and groups in real-world business scenarios.

Best Practices:

- Regularly review and update ledger and group configurations.

- Ensure accurate categorization to maintain clear financial records.
- Avoid redundant or unused ledgers and groups to keep your accounting system streamlined.

Summary: Effectively managing ledgers and groups is crucial for accurate accounting and streamlined financial reporting. Proper setup and maintenance ensure that your financial data is well-organized and easily accessible.

Next Steps: Prepare to delve into voucher entry and other core features in the next chapter, building on the foundation of ledgers and groups management.

This section ensures a comprehensive understanding of creating, managing, and organizing ledgers and groups in Tally, laying the groundwork for efficient and accurate financial management.

2.3   Processing Transactions

Introduction to Transactions

Understanding Transactions:

- Transactions are the backbone of accounting, representing all business activities involving money or value exchange.
- Types of transactions include sales, purchases, payments, receipts, and journal entries.

Voucher Types:

- **Payment Vouchers:** Used to record outgoing payments.

- **Receipt Vouchers:** Used to document incoming funds.
- **Sales Vouchers:** Capture sales transactions.
- **Purchase Vouchers:** Record purchase transactions.
- **Journal Vouchers:** Make general adjustments and transfers.

Recording Transactions

Steps to Record a Voucher:

- **Step 1:** Go to "Accounting Vouchers" in Tally.
- **Step 2:** Select the type of voucher you need to record.
- **Step 3:** Enter the necessary details, such as date, amount, and ledger accounts involved.
- **Step 4:** Save the voucher to finalize the entry.

Best Practices:

- Ensure accuracy by double-checking details before saving.
- Use appropriate narration to provide context for each transaction.

Managing Recurring Transactions

Recurring Vouchers:

- Set up recurring vouchers for transactions that happen regularly, like monthly rent or utility payments.

Automation:

- Utilize Tally's automation features to save time and reduce manual entry errors for recurring transactions.

Adjusting Entries

Journal Entries:

- Use journal vouchers for adjustments that don't fit other voucher types, such as depreciation or accruals.

Importance of Adjusting Entries:

- Ensure accurate financial statements by making necessary adjustments at the end of an accounting period.

Bank Reconciliation

Bank Reconciliation Statement (BRS):

- Match the transactions recorded in Tally with the bank statement to ensure accuracy.

Steps to Reconcile:

- **Step 1:** Access the Bank Reconciliation option.
- **Step 2:** Compare Tally entries with the bank statement.
- **Step 3:** Record any discrepancies and make necessary adjustments.

Handling Errors

Common Errors:

- Identifying typical errors in transaction recording, such as wrong ledger selection or incorrect amounts.

Rectifying Errors:

- Steps to edit or delete incorrect vouchers to maintain accurate records.

Generating Transaction Reports

Transaction Reports:

- Generate reports like Day Book, Cash Book, and Ledger Reports to review transaction history.

Customization:

- Customize reports to fit specific needs, filtering by date, amount, or type of transaction.

Conclusion

Summary:

- Recap of the importance and steps of processing various transactions in Tally.

Next Steps:

- Preparing to explore deeper financial reporting and analysis in subsequent chapters.

This chapter ensures a thorough understanding of processing transactions in Tally, covering everything from recording and managing various types of vouchers to reconciling bank statements and handling errors for accurate and efficient financial management.

> *"Mastering Tally's core features is like unlocking the gears of a well-oiled machine - each function working in harmony to streamline operations and reveal the bigger financial picture."*

CHAPTER 3

Automating Accounting Tasks

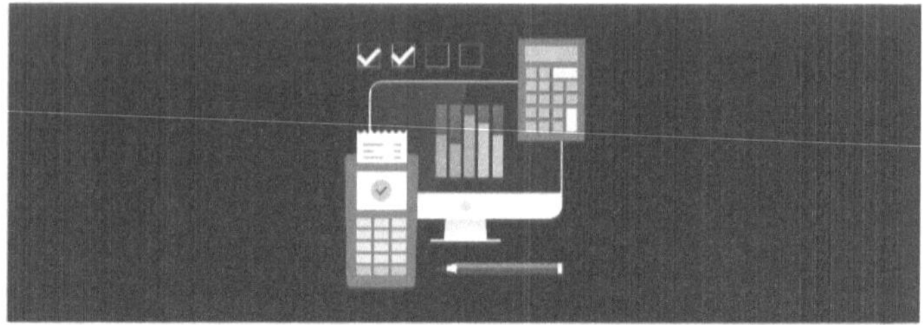

In this chapter, we explore how automation can transform your accounting processes and boost efficiency. We'll delve into Tally's powerful automation features, including automatic data entry, financial report generation, and inventory management. You'll learn how to set up and configure these tools to streamline tasks such as bank reconciliation and payroll processing. We'll also cover how automation helps maintain compliance and troubleshoot common issues. By the end of this chapter, you'll have a clear understanding of how to harness automation to simplify and optimize your accounting practices.

3.1 Utilizing Automation Features

1. Introduction to Automation in Tally

- **Benefits of Automation**

  - The role of automation in reducing manual effort and errors
  - How automation enhances productivity and accuracy in accounting

2. Automating Data Entry

- **Configuring Automatic Data Entry**

  - Setting up data entry templates to standardize and speed up input
  - Using pre-defined formats for recurring transactions (e.g., sales, purchases, expenses)

- **Importing Data**

  - Importing data from external sources (e.g., spreadsheets, other software) to reduce manual entry
  - Validating and integrating imported data into Tally

3. Automating Financial Reports

- **Generating Scheduled Reports**

  - Setting up automated schedules for generating financial reports
  - Customizing report formats and delivery options (e.g., email, print)

- **Automating Report Updates**

  - Configuring automatic updates for reports based on real-time data
  - Ensuring reports reflect the most current financial information

4. Streamlining Transactions with Automation

- **Automating Transaction Entries**

  - Using automation to handle repetitive transaction entries (e.g., recurring invoices, payroll)
  - Configuring rules for automatic transaction postings

- **Integrating with Other Systems**

  - Connecting Tally with other business systems (e.g., CRM, ERP) to automate data synchronization
  - Utilizing APIs and data exchange protocols for seamless integration

5. Managing Inventory with Automation

- **Automated Stock Management**

  - Setting up automated inventory updates based on transactions (e.g., sales, purchases)
  - Configuring alerts for stock levels and reorder points

- **Automating Stock Valuation**

  - Using automation for real-time stock valuation based on chosen methods (e.g., FIFO, LIFO)

6. Automating Compliance and Tax Reporting

- **Configuring Tax Automation**

    - Automating tax calculations and reporting for compliance (e.g., GST, VAT)
    - Setting up rules for tax-related transactions and filings

- **Generating Compliance Reports**

    - Automating the generation of compliance reports and submissions to regulatory bodies

7. Practical Exercise

- **Implementing Automation Features**

    - Hands-on exercise to configure and test various automation features in Tally
    - Setting up automated data entry, reports, and transaction processing based on a sample scenario

This section aims to provide you with a thorough understanding of how to utilize Tally's automation features to streamline accounting processes, enhance efficiency, and ensure accurate financial management.

3.2   Customizing Automation

This section focuses on tailoring Tally's automation features to better suit your business's specific needs. Customizing automation helps streamline processes, ensure accurate data handling, and improve efficiency. Here's an in-depth look at what this chapter entails:

1. Introduction to Customizing Automation

- **Importance of Customization**

  - Customization allows you to align Tally's automation features with your unique business processes and requirements.
  - Tailoring automation can enhance productivity, reduce errors, and ensure that the system addresses your specific operational needs.

2. Customizing Automated Data Entry

- **Creating Custom Templates**

  - **Designing Templates**: Customize templates for recurring transactions such as invoices, purchase orders, and expense reports to include specific fields and information relevant to your business.
  - **Configuring Layouts**: Adjust the layout of these templates to match your business's branding and reporting needs. Include logos, address details, and custom fields as necessary.

- **Defining Data Entry Rules**

  - **Setting Rules**: Establish rules for how data is automatically entered into Tally. For example, set conditions for automatic account postings or tax calculations based on transaction types.
  - **Handling Exceptions**: Customize how Tally handles exceptions or unusual cases in automated entries to ensure accuracy and compliance with your business practices.

3. Tailoring Financial Reports Automation

- **Customizing Report Formats**

  - **Adjusting Formats**: Modify the formats of automated financial reports to meet specific business needs. This includes adding or removing data fields, changing report layouts, and adjusting the level of detail presented.
  - **Creating Custom Reports**: Design custom reports that focus on key performance indicators (KPIs) or specific financial metrics relevant to your business.

- **Configuring Report Schedules**

  - **Setting Schedules**: Create schedules for automated report generation and distribution. Specify the frequency (daily, weekly, monthly) and timing of report generation.
  - **Customizing Delivery**: Configure how and where reports are delivered, such as via email, direct print, or electronic dashboards.

4. Personalizing Transaction Automation

- **Automating Recurring Transactions**

  - **Setting Up Recurring Transactions**: Configure automation for recurring transactions like subscriptions, payroll, or rent payments. Define the frequency, amount, and other relevant details.
  - **Managing Recurrence Rules**: Customize rules for when and how recurring transactions

are posted to ensure they reflect the actual business needs.

- **Managing Transaction Rules**

  - **Defining Rules**: Set up rules for automatic posting of transactions based on specific conditions, such as certain account types or transaction amounts.
  - **Handling Special Cases**: Customize how Tally addresses special or exceptional cases in transactions, ensuring accurate processing and reporting.

5. Customizing Inventory Automation

- **Adjusting Stock Management Settings**

  - **Automating Updates**: Set up automation for updating stock levels based on transactions such as sales and purchases. Define how inventory changes are recorded and reported.
  - **Configuring Alerts**: Customize alerts and notifications for low stock levels, reorder points, or inventory discrepancies to manage stock effectively.

- **Tailoring Stock Valuation Methods**

  - **Selecting Valuation Methods**: Choose and customize stock valuation methods (e.g., FIFO, LIFO, Weighted Average) according to your business requirements.

- o **Automating Valuation**: Configure automation for real-time stock valuation and ensure that stock valuation methods are applied consistently.

6. Adapting Compliance and Tax Automation

- **Customizing Tax Calculations**

  - o **Setting Tax Rules**: Define and customize tax rules and rates specific to your business, including VAT, GST, or other applicable taxes.
  - o **Automating Calculations**: Configure automation for accurate tax calculations and adjustments based on current regulations and business transactions.

- **Modifying Compliance Reporting**

  - o **Tailoring Compliance Reports**: Customize automated compliance reports to meet industry-specific regulatory requirements and standards.
  - o **Adjusting Report Content**: Modify report content and formats to align with regulatory submission requirements and ensure compliance.

7. Practical Exercise

- **Customizing Automation Settings**

  - o **Hands-On Exercise**: Engage in a practical exercise to apply customization techniques in Tally. Create and configure custom templates,

- adjust report formats, and set up automation rules based on a sample business scenario.
  - ○ **Testing Configurations**: Test the customized automation settings to ensure they function correctly and meet your business needs.

This section provides detailed guidance on customizing Tally's automation features, enabling you to tailor the software to your specific business processes and requirements. By the end, you'll be equipped to configure automation settings that enhance accuracy, efficiency, and alignment with your operational needs.

3.3   Practical Exercises for Automation

This section focuses on hands-on exercises to help you apply and master the automation features in Tally. Practical exercises are designed to reinforce your understanding of how to implement and customize automation, ensuring you can effectively streamline your accounting processes. Here's a comprehensive explanation of what you'll cover:

1. Introduction to Practical Exercises

- **Purpose of Exercises**
  - ○ To provide hands-on experience with Tally's automation features
  - ○ To reinforce theoretical knowledge by applying it to real-world scenarios
  - ○ To build confidence in customizing and managing automation in Tally

2. Setting Up Automated Data Entry

- **Exercise: Creating Custom Data Entry Templates**

  - **Objective**: Design and configure custom templates for recurring transactions such as invoices or purchase orders.
  - **Steps**:

    - Access the template creation screen in Tally.
    - Define fields and formats based on business needs.
    - Save and apply the template to simulate data entry for recurring transactions.

- **Exercise: Importing Data**

  - **Objective**: Import data from external sources to automate data entry.
  - **Steps**:

    - Prepare sample data in a spreadsheet or other compatible format.
    - Use Tally's import functionality to load the data.
    - Validate and integrate the imported data into your Tally system.

3. Automating Financial Reports

- **Exercise: Customizing Report Formats**

  - **Objective**: Modify the format of financial reports to suit specific reporting requirements.

- o **Steps**:

    - Access the report customization options in Tally.
    - Adjust fields, layouts, and data presentation according to business needs.
    - Generate and review the customized report to ensure it meets requirements.

- **Exercise: Configuring Report Schedules**

    - o **Objective**: Set up automated schedules for generating and distributing financial reports.
    - o **Steps**:

        - Define the schedule for report generation (e.g., daily, weekly, monthly).
        - Configure delivery options (e.g., email, print).
        - Test the schedule by generating reports and checking distribution.

4. Personalizing Transaction Automation

- **Exercise: Automating Recurring Transactions**

    - o **Objective**: Configure automation for transactions that occur regularly, such as payroll or subscriptions.
    - o **Steps**:

        - Set up recurring transaction templates in Tally.

- Define the frequency, amounts, and other details.
- Simulate the posting of recurring transactions to verify automation.

- **Exercise: Managing Transaction Rules**

  - **Objective**: Establish and customize rules for automatic transaction postings.
  - **Steps**:

    - Define rules for automatic postings based on specific conditions.
    - Configure exceptions and special case handling.
    - Test the rules by entering transactions and observing how they are processed.

5. Customizing Inventory Automation

- **Exercise: Setting Up Automated Stock Updates**

  - **Objective**: Configure Tally to automatically update stock levels based on transactions.
  - **Steps**:

    - Set up automation for stock updates related to sales and purchases.
    - Define inventory management settings and alerts.
    - Perform transactions to test how stock levels are updated automatically.

- **Exercise: Tailoring Stock Valuation Methods**

  - **Objective**: Customize stock valuation methods and automate their application.
  - **Steps**:

    - Choose and configure stock valuation methods (e.g., FIFO, LIFO).
    - Set up automation for real-time valuation updates.
    - Test the system by performing stock-related transactions and reviewing valuation results.

6. Adapting Compliance and Tax Automation

- **Exercise: Configuring Tax Automation**

  - **Objective**: Set up and customize tax rules and calculations for automation.
  - **Steps**:

    - Define tax rates and rules applicable to your business.
    - Configure automation for tax calculations and adjustments.
    - Simulate transactions to ensure accurate tax calculations and reporting.

- **Exercise: Generating Compliance Reports**

  - **Objective**: Automate the creation of compliance reports tailored to regulatory requirements.

- ○ **Steps:**

  - ■ Set up compliance reporting configurations.
  - ■ Customize report formats to meet regulatory standards.
  - ■ Generate and review compliance reports to verify accuracy and completeness.

7. Reviewing and Testing Customizations

- **Exercise: Testing Automated Features**

  - ○ **Objective**: Review and test all customized automation features to ensure they function as intended.
  - ○ **Steps:**

    - ■ Perform end-to-end testing of automated processes.
    - ■ Verify that automation settings and customizations are applied correctly.
    - ■ Troubleshoot and resolve any issues encountered during testing.

8. Conclusion

- **Recap of Practical Skills**

  - ○ Summarize the skills and knowledge gained through the exercises.
  - ○ Highlight the benefits of customizing automation in Tally for efficient accounting management.

- **Next Steps**

  - Encourage ongoing practice and experimentation with Tally's automation features.
  - Suggest further resources or training for advanced customization and automation techniques.

This chapter provides a hands-on approach to mastering Tally's automation features, enabling you to apply theoretical concepts in practical scenarios. By completing these exercises, you'll gain valuable experience in configuring and managing automation to optimize your accounting processes.

"Automation in accounting is not just about saving time; it's about ensuring accuracy, reducing manual effort, and allowing businesses to focus on what truly matters - growth."

CHAPTER 4

Financial Reporting and Analysis

This chapter explores the critical aspects of financial reporting and analysis using Tally. It covers how to generate comprehensive financial reports, analyze financial data for insights, and use reports to drive strategic decision-making. You'll learn to create and customize reports, interpret financial data to assess performance, and leverage insights for effective business management. By the end of this chapter, you'll be adept at utilizing Tally's reporting tools to enhance your financial oversight and strategic planning.

4.1 Generating Financial Reports

This section focuses on how to generate and utilize financial reports in Tally. Financial reports are essential for evaluating the financial health of a business, making informed decisions, and meeting regulatory requirements. You'll learn the various types of reports available, how to generate them, and how to customize them to suit specific needs. Here's a detailed breakdown:

1. Introduction to Financial Reports

- **Importance of Financial Reports**

    - Understanding the role of financial reports in business management
    - How reports provide insights into financial performance and operational efficiency

2. Types of Financial Reports in Tally

- **Balance Sheet**

    - **Purpose**: Shows the financial position of the business at a specific point in time, detailing assets, liabilities, and equity.
    - **Key Components**: Assets (current and fixed), liabilities (current and long-term), owner's equity.

- **Profit and Loss Account (Income Statement)**

    - **Purpose**: Summarizes revenues, costs, and expenses over a specific period to determine net profit or loss.

- o   **Key Components**: Revenue, cost of goods sold, operating expenses, non-operating income and expenses, net profit or loss.

- **Cash Flow Statement**

  - o   **Purpose**: Tracks the flow of cash into and out of the business, showing liquidity and cash management.
  - o   **Key Components**: Operating activities, investing activities, financing activities.

- **Trial Balance**

  - o   **Purpose**: Provides a snapshot of all account balances to verify that debits equal credits.
  - o   **Key Components**: List of all ledger accounts and their balances.

- **Accounts Receivable and Accounts Payable Reports**

  - o   **Purpose**: Details outstanding receivables and payables, helping manage cash flow and credit control.
  - o   **Key Components**: Outstanding invoices, due dates, customer and supplier balances.

3. Generating Reports in Tally

- **Accessing Report Generation**

  - o   **Steps**: Navigate to the Reports section in Tally's main menu.
  - o   **Path**: Gateway of Tally → Display → Financial Statements (or specific report types).

- **Customizing Report Parameters**

  - **Date Range**: Set the period for which you want to generate the report (e.g., monthly, quarterly, annually).
  - **Filters**: Apply filters to focus on specific accounts, cost centers, or transactions.
  - **Formats**: Choose report formats (e.g., detailed, summary) based on your needs.

- **Generating and Viewing Reports**

  - **Steps**: Select the desired report type, configure parameters, and generate the report.
  - **Viewing Options**: Review the report on-screen, export to Excel or PDF, or print directly.

4. Customizing Reports

- **Customizing Report Layouts**

  - **Headers and Footers**: Modify headers and footers to include business name, report title, and date.
  - **Columns and Data Fields**: Adjust columns and data fields to include or exclude specific information.

- **Creating Custom Reports**

  - **Steps**: Use Tally's report customization options to create reports tailored to specific business needs.

- **Templates**: Save customized reports as templates for future use.

- **Configuring Report Schedules**

    - **Automated Scheduling**: Set up schedules for automatically generating and distributing reports at regular intervals.

5. Reviewing and Analyzing Reports

- **Interpreting Report Data**

    - **Key Metrics**: Understand key financial metrics such as profitability, liquidity, and operational efficiency.
    - **Comparison**: Compare current reports with historical data or budgeted figures to assess performance.

- **Identifying Trends and Insights**

    - **Trend Analysis**: Analyze trends over time to identify patterns and make informed decisions.
    - **Insights for Decision-Making**: Use insights from reports to drive strategic planning and operational improvements.

6. Practical Exercise

- **Generating and Customizing Financial Reports**

    - **Objective**: Practice generating various financial reports in Tally and customizing them according to specific needs.

- o **Steps:**

    - Generate a Balance Sheet and Profit and Loss Account for a given period.
    - Customize the report layouts and formats.
    - Review and analyze the reports to draw conclusions and make recommendations.

This section provides a comprehensive guide to generating and customizing financial reports in Tally. By understanding the different types of reports, learning how to generate and customize them, and analyzing the data, you'll be well-equipped to manage and evaluate your business's financial performance effectively.

4.2   Analyzing Financial Data

This section focuses on how to analyze financial data using Tally to gain insights into a business's performance, identify trends, and make informed decisions. Effective analysis helps in understanding financial health, uncovering operational inefficiencies, and strategizing for future growth. Here's a detailed breakdown:

1. Introduction to Financial Data Analysis

- **Importance of Financial Data Analysis**

    - o Understanding how analyzing financial data helps in assessing business performance.
    - o The role of financial analysis in strategic decision-making and operational improvements.

2. Key Financial Metrics and Ratios

- **Profitability Ratios**

    - **Gross Profit Margin**: Measures the percentage of revenue that exceeds the cost of goods sold.

        - **Formula**: (Gross Profit/Revenue) × 100

    - **Net Profit Margin**: Indicates the percentage of revenue remaining after all expenses are deducted.

        - **Formula**: (Net Profit/Revenue) × 100

    - **Return on Assets (ROA)**: Evaluates how efficiently assets are used to generate profit.

        - **Formula**: Net Profit/Total Assets

- **Liquidity Ratios**

    - **Current Ratio**: Assesses the ability to cover short-term liabilities with short-term assets.

        - **Formula**: Current Assets/Current Liabilities

    - **Quick Ratio**: Measures the ability to meet short-term obligations without relying on inventory.

        - **Formula**: (Current Assets – Inventory)/ Current Liabilities

- **Solvency Ratios**

    - **Debt-to-Equity Ratio**: Indicates the proportion of debt used relative to shareholders' equity.

- **Formula**: Total Liabilities/Shareholders' Equity

  ○ **Interest Coverage Ratio**: Measures the ability to pay interest on outstanding debt.

    - **Formula**: Earnings Before Interest and Taxes (EBIT)/Interest Expenses

- **Efficiency Ratios**

  ○ **Inventory Turnover Ratio**: Shows how often inventory is sold and replaced over a period.

    - **Formula**: Cost of Goods Sold/Average Inventory

  ○ **Accounts Receivable Turnover Ratio**: Evaluates how effectively receivables are collected.

    - **Formula**: Net Credit Sales/Average Accounts Receivable

3. Analyzing Financial Reports

- **Analyzing the Balance Sheet**

  ○ **Asset Analysis**: Assess the composition and growth of assets (current vs. fixed).
  ○ **Liability Analysis**: Review the structure of liabilities (short-term vs. long-term) and its implications.
  ○ **Equity Analysis**: Examine changes in owner's equity and retained earnings.

- **Analyzing the Profit and Loss Account**

  - **Revenue Trends**: Analyze revenue streams, growth rates, and seasonality.
  - **Expense Analysis**: Review operating expenses, cost control measures, and variances.
  - **Profitability Trends**: Evaluate changes in profit margins and their causes.

- **Analyzing the Cash Flow Statement**

  - **Operating Cash Flow**: Assess cash generated from core business operations.
  - **Investing Cash Flow**: Review cash used for investments and acquisitions.
  - **Financing Cash Flow**: Examine cash flow from financing activities, including debt and equity changes.

4. Comparative and Trend Analysis

- **Comparative Analysis**

  - **Benchmarking**: Compare financial metrics with industry benchmarks or competitors to evaluate performance.
  - **Historical Comparison**: Analyze financial data over multiple periods to identify trends and changes.

- **Trend Analysis**

  - **Trend Identification**: Identify upward or downward trends in key financial metrics.

- o **Forecasting**: Use historical trends to forecast future financial performance and budget planning.

5. Interpreting Financial Data

- **Drawing Conclusions**

  - o **Performance Evaluation**: Summarize findings from financial reports and ratios to assess overall performance.
  - o **Identifying Strengths and Weaknesses**: Highlight areas of strong performance and areas needing improvement.

- **Making Informed Decisions**

  - o **Strategic Decisions**: Use financial insights to make strategic business decisions, such as investments, cost management, and pricing strategies.
  - o **Operational Improvements**: Identify operational areas that require adjustments based on financial analysis.

6. Practical Exercise

- **Conducting Financial Analysis**

  - o **Objective**: Practice analyzing financial data using Tally's reports and financial ratios.
  - o **Steps**:

    - Generate and review a Balance Sheet, Profit and Loss Account, and Cash Flow Statement.

- Calculate key financial ratios and metrics.
- Perform comparative and trend analysis using historical data.
- Interpret the findings and suggest improvements or strategic actions based on your analysis.

7. Conclusion

- **Recap of Analysis Techniques**

    o Summarize the key techniques and methods for analyzing financial data.
    o Reinforce the importance of accurate analysis for effective business management.

- **Next Steps**

    o Encourage ongoing practice and application of financial analysis techniques.
    o Suggest additional resources or tools for advanced financial analysis and forecasting.

This section provides a thorough guide on analyzing financial data using Tally, equipping you with the skills to evaluate financial performance, identify trends, and make strategic decisions. By mastering these techniques, you'll be able to gain valuable insights into your business's financial health and drive informed decision-making.

4.3   Using Reports for Decision Making

This section explores how to effectively utilize financial reports to inform and guide decision-making within a business. Financial reports provide critical insights into various aspects of business performance, helping leaders make informed strategic and operational decisions. Here's a detailed breakdown of how to use these reports effectively:

1. Introduction to Decision-Making Using Financial Reports

- **Role of Financial Reports in Decision-Making**

    o Understanding how financial reports offer insights into business performance, financial health, and operational efficiency.

    o The importance of using data-driven insights for making strategic and operational decisions.

2. Analyzing Financial Reports for Strategic Decisions

- **Assessing Financial Health**

    o **Balance Sheet Analysis**: Use the balance sheet to evaluate the company's financial position, including asset management, liability structure, and equity status.

    o **Key Insights**: Identify the company's liquidity, solvency, and capital structure to make informed decisions about growth, funding, and risk management.

- **Evaluating Profitability and Efficiency**

    o **Profit and Loss Account Analysis**: Examine revenue, costs, and expenses to assess profitability and operational efficiency.

- o **Key Insights**: Use profitability metrics and cost analysis to make decisions about pricing, cost control, and revenue enhancement strategies.

- **Managing Cash Flow**

  - o **Cash Flow Statement Analysis**: Review cash flows from operating, investing, and financing activities to understand liquidity and cash management.
  - o **Key Insights**: Make decisions about cash reserves, investment opportunities, and financing needs based on cash flow trends.

3. Using Reports to Drive Operational Improvements

- **Identifying Operational Issues**

  - o **Cost and Expense Analysis**: Use financial reports to identify areas of high costs or inefficiencies.
  - o **Key Insights**: Implement cost-saving measures, optimize resource allocation, and improve operational processes based on findings.

- **Performance Monitoring**

  - o **KPIs and Metrics**: Track key performance indicators (KPIs) and financial metrics to monitor ongoing performance.

- o **Key Insights**: Make adjustments to operational strategies and processes based on performance data.

4. Strategic Planning and Forecasting

- **Long-Term Planning**

  - o **Trend Analysis**: Use historical financial data and trend analysis to inform long-term strategic planning.
  - o **Key Insights**: Develop growth strategies, expansion plans, and investment opportunities based on trends and forecasts.

- **Budgeting and Forecasting**

  - o **Budget Creation**: Utilize financial reports to create and adjust budgets that align with business goals and financial projections.
  - o **Key Insights**: Make budgeting decisions based on past performance, current financial status, and future expectations.

5. Decision-Making Scenarios

- **Scenario Analysis**

  - o **Scenario Planning**: Use financial reports to analyze different business scenarios and their potential impact.
  - o **Key Insights**: Make informed decisions by evaluating how various scenarios (e.g., market changes, cost increases) might affect the business.

- **Investment Decisions**

  - **Evaluating Investment Opportunities**: Use financial reports to assess the viability and potential returns of investment opportunities.
  - **Key Insights**: Make decisions about capital allocation, acquisitions, and new projects based on financial performance and projections.

6. Communicating Financial Insights

- **Presenting Financial Data**

  - **Report Presentation**: Effectively communicate financial insights to stakeholders, including management, investors, and board members.
  - **Key Insights**: Use clear and concise presentations to highlight key findings and support decision-making processes.

- **Supporting Decision-Making**

  - **Data-Driven Recommendations**: Provide actionable recommendations based on financial report analysis.
  - **Key Insights**: Use financial data to support strategic initiatives and operational improvements.

7. Practical Exercise

- **Applying Reports for Decision Making**

  - **Objective**: Practice using financial reports to make informed business decisions.

- **Steps**:

    - Generate a set of financial reports (Balance Sheet, Profit and Loss Account, Cash Flow Statement).
    - Analyze the reports to assess financial health, profitability, and cash flow.
    - Develop recommendations for operational improvements, strategic planning, or investment decisions based on the analysis.
    - Present findings and recommendations as if communicating to a business stakeholder or decision-maker.

8. Conclusion

- **Recap of Key Concepts**

    - Summarize the importance of using financial reports for informed decision-making.
    - Reinforce the role of financial analysis in strategic and operational planning.

- **Next Steps**

    - Encourage ongoing practice in analyzing financial reports and applying insights to business decisions.
    - Suggest additional resources for advanced decision-making techniques and financial analysis.

This chapter provides a comprehensive guide to leveraging financial reports for effective decision-making. By understanding how to analyze reports and apply insights, you'll be equipped to make informed strategic and operational decisions that drive business success.

> *"Financial reports are the language of business; mastering their analysis turns data into strategic insights, empowering informed decisions and sustainable success."*

CHAPTER 5

Managing Inventory and Stock

In this chapter, you'll explore the essential techniques for managing inventory and stock effectively using Tally software. Learn how to set up and organize your inventory, track stock movements, and utilize Tally's features to maintain optimal stock levels. This chapter provides practical insights into inventory management methods, recording transactions, and generating insightful reports. By mastering these skills, you'll ensure that your inventory is efficiently managed, helping you to reduce costs and improve overall business performance.

5.1   Setting Up Inventory

Properly setting up inventory in Tally is the foundation for effective stock management. This section will guide you through the steps to configure and organize your inventory system to ensure smooth and accurate tracking of stock.

1. Configuring Inventory Settings:

- **Accessing Inventory Configuration:** Navigate to the Tally Gateway and select "Accounts Info" > "Inventory Info" > "Stock Groups" to start configuring your inventory settings.
- **Creating Stock Groups:** Stock groups help categorize inventory items. Create stock groups based on product categories, departments, or other relevant criteria. For example, you might create groups like "Electronics," "Furniture," or "Raw Materials."
- **Setting Up Stock Categories:** Stock categories allow you to further classify your inventory into specific segments. Define categories such as "Seasonal Items" or "Promotional Stock" to better manage different types of inventory.

2. Creating Stock Items:

- **Adding New Stock Items:** Go to "Stock Item" under "Inventory Info" to create new stock items. Enter details such as the item name, unit of measurement, and opening stock quantity.

- **Defining Item Attributes:** Specify attributes like the item's rate, purchase and sales tax rates, and any additional features such as batch tracking or expiry dates if applicable.

3. Setting Up Units of Measurement:

- **Defining Units of Measurement:** Configure units of measurement (UOM) for your stock items. Tally allows you to set up different units like "Pieces," "Kilograms," or "Liters." This ensures accurate stock tracking and reporting.
- **Creating Unit of Measurement Groups:** If you deal with multiple units for the same item (e.g., "Pieces" and "Boxes"), create unit of measurement groups to handle conversions and maintain consistency in stock records.

4. Stock Valuation Methods:

- **Choosing Valuation Methods:** Tally supports various stock valuation methods like FIFO (First In, First Out), LIFO (Last In, First Out), and Weighted Average. Choose the method that aligns with your business needs and financial practices.
- **Configuring Valuation Settings:** Set up your chosen valuation method in Tally under "Stock Valuation" settings to ensure accurate financial reporting and stock valuation.

5. Managing Stock Transfers:

- **Setting Up Stock Transfer Rules:** Configure rules for transferring stock between different locations or warehouses. This helps in tracking inventory movement and maintaining accurate stock levels across multiple sites.

- **Recording Stock Transfers:** Enter stock transfer transactions in Tally to reflect movement between locations. Ensure that all transfers are recorded accurately to avoid discrepancies.

6. Regular Review and Updates:

- **Reviewing Inventory Setup:** Periodically review your inventory setup to ensure it meets current business needs. Update stock groups, items, and categories as necessary to reflect changes in inventory or business operations.
- **Maintaining Accurate Records:** Regularly audit inventory records to ensure accuracy. Address any discrepancies promptly to maintain reliable stock information.

By following these steps, you'll establish a robust inventory management system in Tally that supports efficient tracking, accurate valuation, and streamlined operations.

5.2   Tracking Stock Movements

Accurately tracking stock movements is vital for effective inventory management. This section covers how to monitor and record the flow of inventory items through various transactions, ensuring you maintain precise stock levels and minimize discrepancies.

1. Recording Purchases:

- **Entering Purchase Entries:** Use Tally to record inventory purchases accurately. Navigate to "Purchase Voucher" and enter details such as the supplier's name, item descriptions, quantities, rates, and applicable taxes. Ensure that the purchase entries are correctly categorized under relevant stock groups and units of measurement.

- **Handling Purchase Returns:** Record purchase returns using the "Purchase Return Voucher" to adjust stock levels when items are returned to suppliers. This will help in maintaining accurate inventory records and ensure that stock quantities reflect returns appropriately.

2. Managing Sales Transactions:

- **Recording Sales Entries:** Enter sales transactions in Tally under "Sales Voucher." Provide details like the customer's name, items sold, quantities, rates, and taxes. Ensure that the sales are recorded under the correct stock groups and units to accurately track stock depletion.

- **Handling Sales Returns:** Use the "Sales Return Voucher" to record returns from customers. This adjustment helps in maintaining accurate stock levels and reflecting returns in your inventory records.

3. Tracking Stock Adjustments:

- **Recording Stock Adjustments:** Adjust stock levels to account for discrepancies, damages, or spoilage using the "Stock Journal" or "Stock Adjustment

Voucher." Enter the nature of the adjustment, item details, quantities, and reasons for the change.

- **Managing Inventory Losses and Gains:** Document inventory losses or gains through adjustment entries to ensure that stock records match actual inventory levels. This helps in reconciling physical stock counts with recorded quantities.

4. Managing Stock Transfers:

- **Recording Internal Transfers:** Use Tally to record transfers of stock between different locations or warehouses. Go to "Stock Transfer Voucher" and enter details such as source and destination locations, items being transferred, and quantities.
- **Tracking Transfer Documentation:** Ensure that each stock transfer is documented with proper references and supporting information. This will help in tracking the movement of stock and maintaining accurate inventory records.

5. Utilizing Inventory Reports:

- **Generating Stock Movement Reports:** Leverage Tally's reporting features to generate reports on stock movements. Reports like "Stock Summary," "Stock Item Movement," and "Stock Journal" provide insights into inventory flow and help identify trends or issues.
- **Customizing Reports:** Customize reports to focus on specific aspects of stock movements, such as by date range, stock group, or location. This helps in analyzing inventory performance and making informed decisions.

6. Conducting Regular Stock Audits:

- **Performing Physical Stock Counts:** Regularly conduct physical stock audits to verify the accuracy of recorded inventory levels. Compare physical counts with Tally records to identify discrepancies and make necessary adjustments.
- **Reconciliation Procedures:** Reconcile differences between physical counts and recorded stock levels. Investigate and resolve discrepancies to ensure that inventory records are accurate and reliable.

7. Best Practices for Accurate Tracking:

- **Implementing Inventory Controls:** Establish controls and procedures to manage stock movements effectively. Implement checks and balances to prevent errors and ensure accurate recording of transactions.
- **Training and Awareness:** Train staff involved in inventory management on best practices and Tally procedures. Ensure that everyone understands the importance of accurate stock tracking and follows established protocols.

By following these steps, you'll be able to track stock movements efficiently, ensuring accurate inventory records and effective management of stock levels.

5.3   Generating Inventory Reports

Generating inventory reports is essential for monitoring stock performance, analyzing trends, and making informed business decisions. This section outlines how to effectively use Tally to generate and customize various inventory reports, ensuring you have the insights needed for effective inventory management.

1. Accessing Inventory Reports in Tally:

- **Navigating to Reports:** Go to the Tally Gateway of Tally and select "Display" > "Inventory Books" to access the range of inventory reports available.
- **Choosing Report Types:** Tally offers various types of inventory reports. Choose the appropriate report based on the information you need, such as stock summaries, item movements, or valuations.

2. Generating Stock Summary Reports:

- **Overview of Stock Summary:** The Stock Summary report provides a snapshot of your inventory levels, including details on current stock quantities, valuations, and stock status.
- **Customizing Stock Summary:** Customize the Stock Summary report to filter by stock group, item, location, or date range. This helps in obtaining specific insights and focusing on particular aspects of your inventory.

3. Analyzing Stock Item Movements:

- **Understanding Item Movement Reports:** The Stock Item Movement report tracks the inflow and outflow of individual stock items over a specified period. It includes details such as purchase and sales quantities, adjustments, and stock levels.
- **Filtering and Customizing Movements:** Filter the report by stock item, group, or location to get detailed

insights into specific items or segments. Customize the date range to analyze movement trends over different periods.

4. Utilizing Stock Journal Reports:

- **Purpose of Stock Journal Reports:** Stock Journal reports capture all stock-related transactions, including adjustments, transfers, and other inventory changes. This report helps in reviewing detailed inventory movements and adjustments.
- **Generating and Analyzing Journals:** Generate Stock Journal reports to review entries and ensure accuracy. Analyze the journal to identify any discrepancies or unusual stock movements that may require further investigation.

5. Generating Valuation Reports:

- **Overview of Valuation Reports:** Valuation reports provide insights into the monetary value of your inventory based on the chosen valuation method (FIFO, LIFO, Weighted Average). They help in understanding the financial impact of stock levels.
- **Customizing Valuation Reports:** Customize valuation reports to reflect different stock groups, items, or locations. This enables you to assess the value of inventory accurately and make informed financial decisions.

6. Customizing Reports for Business Needs:

- **Using Filters and Parameters:** Tally allows you to apply filters and set parameters to tailor reports according to specific business requirements. Adjust filters such as date ranges, stock groups, or locations to focus on relevant data.

- **Creating and Saving Custom Reports:** Create customized reports that cater to your specific reporting needs. Save these customizations for future use to streamline reporting processes and ensure consistency.

7. Exporting and Sharing Reports:

- **Exporting Reports:** Tally provides options to export reports in various formats, including PDF, Excel, or HTML. Exporting reports allows for easy sharing and further analysis outside of Tally.
- **Sharing Insights:** Share generated reports with stakeholders or team members to provide insights into inventory performance. Ensure that reports are clear, accurate, and relevant to the intended audience.

8. Best Practices for Reporting:

- **Regular Report Generation:** Schedule regular report generation to stay updated on inventory status and performance. This helps in proactive management and timely decision-making.
- **Review and Interpretation:** Regularly review generated reports and interpret the data to identify trends, issues, or opportunities for improvement. Use insights gained from reports to make informed inventory management decisions.

By effectively generating and analyzing inventory reports in Tally, you'll gain valuable insights into your inventory operations, helping you manage stock levels efficiently and make data-driven decisions.

> *"Efficient inventory management is the cornerstone of profitability. When stock is tracked and optimized, businesses gain control over their operations and unlock true potential."*

CHAPTER 6

Payroll Management

This chapter explores the fundamentals of managing payroll using Tally software. Learn how to efficiently process employee salaries, track deductions, and ensure compliance with tax regulations. With practical guidance on setting up payroll configurations, handling various pay components, and generating payroll reports, this chapter equips you with the tools to streamline payroll processes and maintain accurate and timely employee compensation.

6.1 Configuring Payroll Settings

Properly configuring payroll settings in Tally is essential for accurate and efficient payroll management. This section provides a step-by-step guide to setting up payroll configurations to ensure that employee compensation is managed correctly and in compliance with relevant regulations.

1. Activating Payroll Features:

- **Enabling Payroll:** To start using payroll features in Tally, you need to activate payroll functionality. Go to "Gateway of Tally" > "F11: Features" > "F1: Accounting Features" and set "Maintain Payroll" to "Yes."

- **Configuring Payroll Settings:** Once payroll is activated, access "Payroll Info" under "Accounts Info" to configure the necessary payroll settings, including salary components and statutory deductions.

2. Creating Payroll Masters:

- **Setting Up Employee Groups:** Define employee groups based on categories such as departments or job roles. Navigate to "Payroll Info" > "Employee Groups" to create and manage these groups.

- **Adding Employee Details:** Enter employee details under "Payroll Info" > "Employees" by creating new employee records. Include essential information such as name, designation, department, salary structure, and bank details for direct deposits.

- **Defining Pay Structures:** Configure pay structures by setting up salary components. Go to "Payroll

Info" > "Salary Details" and define components such as basic salary, allowances, bonuses, and deductions.

3. Configuring Salary Components:

- **Creating Salary Components:** Create salary components under "Payroll Info" > "Salary Components." Define each component's type (e.g., earnings, deductions) and specify calculation methods, such as fixed amounts or percentages.
- **Setting Component Parameters:** Configure parameters for each salary component, including whether it's taxable or non-taxable, and set up any applicable formulas for calculation.

4. Setting Up Statutory Deductions:

- **Configuring Tax Deductions:** Set up statutory deductions like Income Tax (TDS) and Provident Fund (PF) under "Payroll Info" > "Statutory Deductions." Define the applicable rules and rates based on the relevant regulations.
- **Managing Other Deductions:** Include any other mandatory or voluntary deductions, such as loan repayments or insurance premiums, by adding them as separate components in the payroll settings.

5. Establishing Payroll Periods:

- **Defining Payroll Periods:** Set up payroll periods to determine how frequently payroll is processed (e.g., monthly, bi-weekly). Configure these periods under "Payroll Info" > "Payroll Periods."

- **Handling Partial Periods:** If needed, configure settings to handle payroll for partial periods, such as when employees join or leave in the middle of a payroll cycle.

6. Configuring Payroll Reports:

- **Setting Up Report Parameters:** Customize report parameters to suit your organization's needs. Configure settings to include necessary details in payroll reports, such as employee names, salary components, and deductions.
- **Generating Sample Reports:** Generate sample payroll reports to ensure that the configurations are accurate. Review the reports to confirm that all components and deductions are calculated correctly.

7. Review and Testing:

- **Testing Payroll Setup:** Conduct a test run of the payroll process to verify that all settings and calculations are functioning as intended. Review the results and make any necessary adjustments.
- **Reviewing Configurations:** Regularly review payroll settings to ensure they remain accurate and compliant with any changes in regulations or organizational policies.

By thoroughly configuring payroll settings in Tally, you'll create a solid foundation for accurate and efficient payroll management, ensuring that employee compensation is handled correctly and in compliance with statutory requirements.

6.2   Processing Payroll

Processing payroll involves calculating and disbursing employee salaries accurately, considering all relevant salary components, deductions, and statutory requirements. This section provides a comprehensive guide to executing payroll in Tally, ensuring timely and correct salary payments.

1. Preparing Payroll Data:

- **Collecting Attendance Records:** Gather attendance data, including working hours, leaves, and overtime, which will be used to calculate employee salaries. Ensure that attendance records are accurate and up-to-date.
- **Updating Employee Information:** Verify that all employee records are current, including salary details, allowances, and deductions. Update any changes such as promotions, salary increments, or new hires.

2. Generating Payroll Vouchers:

- **Accessing Payroll Vouchers:** Navigate to "Gateway of Tally" > "Payroll Vouchers" to start the payroll processing. Choose the appropriate voucher type based on the payroll period (e.g., monthly).
- **Entering Payroll Details:** Enter payroll details for each employee, including the salary components, deductions, and any adjustments. Ensure that all components are correctly calculated based on the configured salary structures.

3. Calculating Salaries:

- **Automatic Calculation:** Tally calculates salaries automatically based on the configured salary components and employee details. Verify the calculations to ensure accuracy.
- **Handling Adjustments:** Make any necessary adjustments for bonuses, deductions, or corrections. Record these adjustments in the payroll voucher to ensure that they are reflected in the final salary calculation.

4. Processing Statutory Deductions:

- **Calculating Deductions:** Tally will automatically calculate statutory deductions such as Income Tax (TDS), Provident Fund (PF), and Professional Tax based on the configured rules and employee details.
- **Ensuring Compliance:** Review deductions to ensure compliance with regulatory requirements. Adjust deduction settings as necessary to meet any changes in tax laws or statutory regulations.

5. Generating Pay Slips:

- **Creating Pay Slips:** Generate pay slips for each employee using Tally's "Pay Slip" feature. Pay slips provide a detailed breakdown of salary components, deductions, and net pay.
- **Distributing Pay Slips:** Distribute pay slips to employees, either electronically or in printed form. Ensure that employees review their pay slips for accuracy and address any discrepancies.

6. Processing Payments:

- **Recording Payments:** Record salary payments using Tally's "Payment Voucher" or "Bank Payment" feature. Enter details such as payment amounts, bank accounts, and payment methods.
- **Handling Bank Transfers:** For direct bank transfers, ensure that payment details match the amounts and bank account information recorded in Tally.

7. Generating Payroll Reports:

- **Creating Payroll Reports:** Use Tally's reporting features to generate reports such as "Payroll Summary," "Salary Register," and "Deduction Report." These reports provide insights into payroll expenses, deductions, and overall salary distribution.
- **Reviewing and Analyzing Reports:** Review generated reports to verify accuracy and ensure that payroll data aligns with company records. Use reports to analyze payroll expenses and make informed decisions.

8. Compliance and Record-Keeping:

- **Maintaining Records:** Ensure that all payroll records, including pay slips, vouchers, and statutory deduction details, are accurately maintained and easily accessible for audit purposes.
- **Compliance Checks:** Regularly check compliance with employment laws and regulations. Update payroll settings and processes as needed to adhere to any changes in statutory requirements.

<u>9. Finalizing Payroll:</u>

- **Review and Approval:** Conduct a final review of the payroll entries and calculations before finalizing. Obtain necessary approvals from relevant authorities or departments.

- **Closing Payroll Period:** Once payroll is finalized, close the payroll period in Tally to prevent further modifications. This ensures that payroll records are locked and secure for that period.

By following these steps, you will efficiently process payroll in Tally, ensuring accurate salary payments, compliance with statutory requirements, and effective management of payroll data.

6.3 Payroll Reports and Compliance

Effective payroll management not only involves processing salaries but also ensuring compliance with regulatory requirements and generating accurate reports. This section provides a guide to generating payroll reports, understanding their significance, and maintaining compliance with statutory regulations.

<u>1. Generating Payroll Reports:</u>

- **Accessing Payroll Reports:** Go to "Gateway of Tally" > "Display" > "Payroll Reports" to access the various payroll reports available in Tally. Select the relevant report based on your needs.

- **Types of Payroll Reports:**

  - **Payroll Summary Report:** Provides an overview of total salary expenses, including breakdowns by employee, department, or cost center.

- o **Salary Register Report:** Lists detailed salary information for each employee, including salary components, deductions, and net pay.
- o **Deduction Report:** Shows details of statutory and other deductions made from employee salaries, such as Income Tax (TDS) and Provident Fund (PF).
- o **Pay Slip Report:** Generates individual pay slips for employees, showing a detailed breakdown of earnings, deductions, and net salary.

- **Customizing Reports:** Customize reports by setting filters for date ranges, employee groups, departments, or other parameters. This helps in focusing on specific data and generating relevant insights.

2. Analyzing Payroll Reports:

- **Reviewing Salary Distribution:** Analyze reports to understand salary distribution across the organization. Review details such as average salaries, highest and lowest pay, and overall payroll expenses.
- **Monitoring Deductions:** Check deduction reports to ensure accuracy and compliance with statutory requirements. Verify that all deductions are correctly applied and calculated.
- **Assessing Compliance:** Use reports to assess compliance with legal and regulatory requirements. Ensure that statutory deductions and contributions are accurately reported and paid.

3. Ensuring Compliance:

- **Understanding Legal Requirements:** Familiarize yourself with legal requirements related to payroll, including tax regulations, provident fund contributions, and other statutory obligations.
- **Maintaining Accurate Records:** Keep detailed records of payroll transactions, including salary payments, deductions, and contributions. Accurate record-keeping is essential for compliance and audit purposes.
- **Filing Statutory Returns:** Ensure timely filing of statutory returns and payments, such as Income Tax (TDS) returns and Provident Fund (PF) contributions. Use Tally's reporting features to generate the necessary reports and documentation for filings.

4. Handling Statutory Compliance:

- **Income Tax (TDS) Compliance:** Ensure that TDS is calculated and deducted as per applicable tax slabs and rules. Generate TDS reports and file returns in compliance with tax regulations.
- **Provident Fund (PF) Compliance:** Verify that PF contributions are accurately calculated and deducted. Generate PF reports and ensure timely submission of PF returns.
- **Professional Tax Compliance:** For regions with professional tax requirements, ensure that professional tax is deducted and reported correctly. Generate relevant reports and comply with regional regulations.

5. Audits and Reconciliation:

- **Conducting Internal Audits:** Regularly perform internal audits of payroll records to identify discrepancies or errors. Ensure that all payroll transactions are accurately recorded and reconciled.
- **Reconciliation with Bank Statements:** Reconcile payroll payments with bank statements to verify that salary payments have been processed correctly. Address any discrepancies promptly.

6. Reviewing and Updating Payroll Processes:

- **Regular Review:** Periodically review payroll processes and reports to ensure they are effective and compliant with current regulations. Update processes as needed based on changes in laws or organizational policies.
- **Training and Awareness:** Train payroll staff on compliance requirements and reporting procedures. Ensure they are aware of any changes in regulations and how to implement them in Tally.

By generating comprehensive payroll reports and maintaining compliance with statutory requirements, you'll ensure accurate payroll management and uphold regulatory standards, contributing to effective and lawful business operations.

"An efficient payroll system is the backbone of employee satisfaction and business stability. When done right, it ensures that everyone's efforts are valued and accounted for."

CHAPTER 7

Taxation and Compliance

This chapter delves into the intricacies of managing taxation and ensuring compliance using Tally software. Learn how to handle various tax obligations, including Goods and Services Tax (GST), Income Tax, and other statutory requirements. Gain insights into configuring tax settings, generating compliance reports, and adhering to regulatory standards to ensure accurate tax reporting and timely submissions.

7.1   Setting Up Taxation

Taxation is a critical aspect of business accounting. Properly setting up taxation in Tally can streamline financial operations and ensure compliance with legal requirements. This chapter will guide you through the step-by-step process of configuring taxation settings in Tally to handle various tax scenarios efficiently.

Overview of Taxation in Tally

Before diving into the setup process, it's essential to understand the types of taxes commonly managed in Tally:

1. **Goods and Services Tax (GST)**: A comprehensive indirect tax levied on the manufacture, sale, and consumption of goods and services.
2. **Income Tax**: Direct tax imposed on the income of individuals and businesses.
3. **Withholding Tax (TDS/TCS)**: Tax deducted at source or collected at source, applicable to specific transactions.
4. **Other Taxes**: Such as Professional Tax, Property Tax, etc.

Step-by-Step Guide to Setting Up Taxation

Step 1: Enable Tax Features in Tally

1. **Open Tally ERP 9**:

    ○   Navigate to Gateway of Tally.
    ○   Select F11: Features and then F3: Statutory & Taxation.

2. **Activate Taxation:**

    o   Set Enable Goods and Services Tax (GST) to Yes.

    o   Set Enable Tax Deducted at Source (TDS) to Yes.

    o   Set Enable Tax Collected at Source (TCS) to Yes.

    o   Enable other relevant tax features as needed.

Step 2: Configure GST Details

1. **Company GST Details:**

    o   Go to Gateway of Tally.

    o   Select F12: Configure and then GST.

    o   Enter the company's GSTIN (Goods and Services Tax Identification Number).

    o   Fill in the applicable GST rates for different items.

2. **Create GST Ledgers:**

    o   Navigate to Accounts Info > Ledgers > Create.

    o   Create ledgers for Central Tax, State Tax, Integrated Tax, and Cess.

    o   Specify the appropriate tax percentage for each ledger.

Step 3: Set Up TDS

1. **TDS Deductors and Deductees:**

    o   Go to Gateway of Tally > Masters > Statutory Info > TDS Nature of Payment.

- Create TDS nature of payments, specifying the applicable section and tax rate.

2. **Create TDS Ledgers**:

   - Navigate to Accounts Info > Ledgers > Create.
   - Create TDS ledgers for TDS Payable and TDS Receivable.

Step 4: Configure TCS

1. **TCS Categories**:

   - Go to Gateway of Tally > Masters > Statutory Info > TCS Nature of Payment.
   - Create TCS categories, specifying the applicable section and tax rate.

2. **Create TCS Ledgers**:

   - Navigate to Accounts Info > Ledgers > Create.
   - Create TCS ledgers for TCS Payable and TCS Receivable.

Step 5: Set Up Other Taxes

1. **Professional Tax**:

   - Go to Gateway of Tally > Masters > Statutory Info > Professional Tax.
   - Create professional tax categories and define the applicable rates.

2. **Property Tax and Others**:

   - Create ledgers for any other taxes applicable to your business.

- Define the tax percentage and relevant details for each ledger.

Practical Example: Setting Up GST for a Product Sale

1. **Create a Sales Ledger:**

   - Go to Accounts Info > Ledgers > Create.
   - Name it Sales and under Under select Sales Accounts.
   - Set Is GST Applicable to Yes and select the appropriate tax rate.

2. **Create a Purchase Ledger:**

   - Go to Accounts Info > Ledgers > Create.
   - Name it Purchases and under Under select Purchase Accounts.
   - Set Is GST Applicable to Yes and select the appropriate tax rate.

3. **Record a Sale Transaction:**

   - Navigate to Gateway of Tally > Accounting Vouchers.
   - Select F8: Sales.
   - Enter the relevant details, including the customer, items sold, and applicable GST.

4. **Verify Tax Calculations:**

   - After recording the transaction, review the GST ledgers to ensure the correct amounts are posted.

Tips for Efficient Taxation Management

- **Regular Updates**: Keep your Tally software updated to ensure compliance with the latest tax laws and regulations.
- **Accurate Data Entry**: Ensure all details, such as GSTIN, PAN, and tax rates, are correctly entered to avoid discrepancies.
- **Periodic Audits**: Regularly audit your tax transactions to ensure accuracy and compliance.
- **Training**: Keep your accounting team trained on the latest tax regulations and Tally features.

Setting up taxation in Tally may seem complex, but following these steps ensures a smooth and compliant process. Properly configured tax settings not only streamline your accounting processes but also help in avoiding legal complications. This section has provided a comprehensive guide to setting up various taxes in Tally, preparing you for efficient tax management.

7.2   Calculating and Reporting Taxes

Accurate tax calculation and timely reporting are crucial for maintaining compliance and avoiding penalties. This chapter will guide you through the processes of calculating taxes in Tally, generating necessary reports, and ensuring your business adheres to statutory requirements.

Overview of Tax Calculation in Tally

Tally ERP 9 automates tax calculations for various types of taxes, including GST, TDS, and TCS. This automation ensures precision and saves time, allowing you to focus on other critical aspects of your business.

Step-by-Step Guide to Calculating Taxes

Step 1: Calculating GST

1. **Record Transactions**:

    o   Ensure all sales and purchase transactions are recorded accurately in Tally.

    o   Navigate to Gateway of Tally > Accounting Vouchers.

    o   Select F8: Sales or F9: Purchase and enter the transaction details, including GST rates.

2. **Verify GST Calculations**:

    o   After recording the transactions, verify that the GST calculations are accurate.

    o   Go to Gateway of Tally > Display > Statutory Reports > GST Reports.

    o   Review reports like GSTR-1 (Outward Supplies), GSTR-2 (Inward Supplies), and GSTR-3B (Summary Return) for accuracy.

Step 2: Calculating TDS

1. **Record Transactions**:

    o   Record transactions involving TDS using the appropriate vouchers.

    o   Navigate to Gateway of Tally > Accounting Vouchers.

- o Select F7: Journal or F4: Contra and enter the transaction details, ensuring TDS is applied.

2. **Verify TDS Calculations**:

   - o Go to Gateway of Tally > Display > Statutory Reports > TDS Reports.
   - o Review reports like TDS Computation, Form 26Q, and Form 27Q to ensure accuracy.

Step 3: Calculating TCS

1. **Record Transactions**:

   - o Record transactions involving TCS using the appropriate vouchers.
   - o Navigate to Gateway of Tally > Accounting Vouchers.
   - o Select F8: Sales and enter the transaction details, ensuring TCS is applied.

2. **Verify TCS Calculations**:

   - o Go to Gateway of Tally > Display > Statutory Reports > TCS Reports.
   - o Review reports like TCS Computation, Form 27EQ, and Form 27D to ensure accuracy.

<u>Step-by-Step Guide to Reporting Taxes</u>

Step 1: Generating GST Reports

1. **GSTR-1 Report**:

   - o Navigate to Gateway of Tally > Display > Statutory Reports > GST Reports > GSTR-1.

- o This report shows details of outward supplies (sales) and helps in filing the GSTR-1 return.

2. **GSTR-2 Report:**

- o Go to Gateway of Tally > Display > Statutory Reports > GST Reports > GSTR-2.
- o This report shows details of inward supplies (purchases) and helps in filing the GSTR-2 return.

3. **GSTR-3B Report:**

- o Navigate to Gateway of Tally > Display > Statutory Reports > GST Reports > GSTR-3B.
- o This summary return report helps in monthly GST filings.

Step 2: Generating TDS Reports

1. **TDS Computation Report:**

- o Go to Gateway of Tally > Display > Statutory Reports > TDS Reports > TDS Computation.
- o This report shows the computation of TDS for various deductees and helps in filing TDS returns.

2. **Form 26Q and 27Q:**

- o Navigate to Gateway of Tally > Display > Statutory Reports > TDS Reports > Form 26Q or Form 27Q.

- ○ These forms are used for filing quarterly TDS returns for resident and non-resident payments, respectively.

Step 3: Generating TCS Reports

1. **TCS Computation Report**:

   - ○ Go to Gateway of Tally > Display > Statutory Reports > TCS Reports > TCS Computation.
   - ○ This report shows the computation of TCS for various collectees and helps in filing TCS returns.

2. **Form 27EQ and 27D**:

   - ○ Navigate to Gateway of Tally > Display > Statutory Reports > TCS Reports > Form 27EQ or Form 27D.
   - ○ These forms are used for filing quarterly TCS returns and issuing TCS certificates, respectively.

<u>Practical Example: Generating a GSTR-3B Report</u>

1. **Access GSTR-3B**:

   - ○ Go to Gateway of Tally > Display > Statutory Reports > GST Reports > GSTR-3B.

2. **Review the Report**:

   - ○ Check the summary of outward and inward supplies.
   - ○ Verify the tax liabilities and input tax credits.

3. **Export the Report**:

   o   Click on E: Export to save the report in the required format.

   o   Use the exported report to file your monthly GSTR-3B return on the GST portal.

<u>Tips for Efficient Tax Calculation and Reporting</u>

- **Regular Reconciliation**: Regularly reconcile your ledgers with tax reports to ensure accuracy.
- **Stay Updated**: Keep yourself updated with the latest tax regulations and ensure Tally is configured accordingly.
- **Automate Where Possible**: Use Tally's automation features to reduce manual errors and save time.
- **Seek Professional Help**: Consult with a tax professional for complex tax scenarios and ensure compliance.

Efficient tax calculation and reporting are vital for the smooth operation of any business. By leveraging Tally's robust features, you can automate these processes, ensuring accuracy and compliance. This section has provided a detailed guide to calculating and reporting various taxes in Tally.

7.3   Ensuring Compliance

Compliance with tax regulations and statutory requirements is crucial for any business. Non-compliance can result in penalties, legal issues, and damage to your business reputation. This section will guide you through the best practices for ensuring compliance in Tally, including setting up audit trails, generating statutory reports, and staying updated with regulatory changes.

Overview of Compliance in Tally

Tally ERP 9 offers a comprehensive suite of tools to help businesses comply with various tax laws and statutory requirements. These tools include audit features, statutory reports, and automatic updates for the latest tax rules.

Step-by-Step Guide to Ensuring Compliance

Step 1: Set Up Audit Trails

1. **Enable Audit Features**:

   - Navigate to Gateway of Tally.
   - Select F11: Features and then F3: Statutory & Taxation.
   - Enable Use Audit Features to Yes.

2. **Configure Audit Logs**:

   - Go to Gateway of Tally > Audit & Compliance.
   - Set up audit logs to track changes in transactions and master data.

3. **Review Audit Trails**:

   - Regularly review audit trails to identify and rectify discrepancies.
   - Navigate to Gateway of Tally > Audit & Compliance > Audit Logs.

Step 2: Generate Statutory Reports

1. **GST Reports**:

   o Navigate to Gateway of Tally > Display > Statutory Reports > GST Reports.
   o Generate GSTR-1, GSTR-2, and GSTR-3B reports for GST compliance.

2. **TDS and TCS Reports**:

   o Go to Gateway of Tally > Display > Statutory Reports > TDS Reports or TCS Reports.
   o Generate Form 26Q, 27Q, 27EQ, and other relevant TDS/TCS reports.

3. **Other Statutory Reports**:

   o Generate reports for Professional Tax, Employee Provident Fund (EPF), Employee State Insurance (ESI), etc.
   o Navigate to Gateway of Tally > Display > Statutory Reports and select the relevant report type.

Step 3: Reconcile Accounts Regularly

1. **Bank Reconciliation**:

   o Go to Gateway of Tally > Banking > Bank Reconciliation.
   o Reconcile bank statements with ledger entries to ensure accuracy.

2. **GST Reconciliation**:

   - Navigate to Gateway of Tally > Display > Statutory Reports > GST Reports > GSTR-2A Reconciliation.
   - Match your purchase data with supplier data to claim accurate input tax credits.

3. **Vendor and Customer Reconciliation**:

   - Regularly reconcile accounts with vendors and customers to ensure accuracy.
   - Navigate to Gateway of Tally > Display > Account Books > Ledger.

Step 4: Stay Updated with Regulatory Changes

1. **Automatic Updates**:

   - Ensure Tally ERP 9 is set to receive automatic updates.
   - Navigate to Gateway of Tally > F12: Configure > General and enable Automatic Updates.

2. **Consult Tax Professionals**:

   - Regularly consult with tax professionals to stay updated on the latest regulatory changes.
   - Implement changes in Tally as per their advice.

Step 5: Conduct Regular Audits

1. **Internal Audits**:

   - Conduct regular internal audits to ensure all transactions are accurately recorded and compliant.

- o Use Tally's audit features to assist in this process.

2. **External Audits**:

    - o Hire external auditors to conduct periodic audits and provide an unbiased review of your compliance status.
    - o Provide auditors with access to necessary Tally reports and data.

Practical Example: Conducting a GST Reconciliation

1. **Access GSTR-2A Reconciliation**:

    - o Navigate to Gateway of Tally > Display > Statutory Reports > GST Reports > GSTR-2A Reconciliation.

2. **Match Purchase Data**:

    - o Compare your purchase invoices with the data available in the GSTR-2A report.
    - o Identify mismatches and rectify them by contacting suppliers or making necessary adjustments.

3. **Finalize Input Tax Credit (ITC)**:

    - o Ensure all eligible input tax credits are claimed accurately.
    - o Save and export the reconciled report for filing.

Tips for Ensuring Compliance

- **Regular Monitoring**: Monitor transactions and reports regularly to catch discrepancies early.
- **Training**: Keep your accounting team trained on the latest compliance requirements and Tally features.
- **Documentation**: Maintain proper documentation for all transactions to support your compliance efforts.
- **Automate**: Utilize Tally's automation features to reduce manual errors and enhance compliance.

Conclusion

Ensuring compliance is a continuous process that requires diligence and regular updates. By leveraging Tally's features, you can streamline compliance activities, reduce risks, and focus on growing your business. This chapter has provided a detailed guide to setting up audit trails, generating statutory reports, and staying updated with regulatory changes to ensure your business remains compliant.

"Understanding and managing taxes is the key to unlocking financial efficiency. Compliance is not a burden but a bridge to sustainable growth and business credibility."

CHAPTER 8

Troubleshooting and Best Practices

Ensuring smooth operation and optimal performance of Tally requires not only a good understanding of its features but also the ability to troubleshoot common issues and implement best practices. This chapter provides a concise guide to identifying and resolving frequent problems in Tally, as well as key best practices that can help maintain data integrity and enhance efficiency. Whether you're dealing with data corruption, slow performance, or GST calculation errors, this chapter will equip you with the knowledge to address these challenges effectively.

8.1   Common Issues and Solutions

In the course of using Tally, users may encounter various issues that can disrupt workflow and data integrity. This chapter focuses on common problems faced in Tally and provides detailed solutions to troubleshoot and resolve these issues. Addressing these problems promptly and effectively ensures the smooth functioning of your accounting operations.

1. Data Corruption

Symptoms:

- Errors during data entry
- Sudden application crashes
- Data inconsistencies

Solutions:

1. **Rewriting Company Data**:

     o   Navigate to Gateway of Tally > Company Info > Rewrite Company Data.

     o   Select the company and confirm the rewrite process. This can fix minor data corruptions.

2. **Backup and Restore**:

- Restore data from the latest backup if corruption is severe.
- Ensure regular backups to prevent significant data loss.

2. Slow Performance

Symptoms:

- Lagging or slow response times

Solutions:

1. **Data Optimization**:

- Periodically split company data: Gateway of Tally > Alt+F3 > Split Company Data.
- Archive old data to reduce load.

2. **System Requirements**:

- Ensure your system meets Tally's hardware and software requirements.
- Upgrade RAM and storage if necessary.

3. GST Calculation Errors

Symptoms:

- Incorrect tax calculations
- Mismatched GST reports

Solutions:

1. **Verify GST Settings:**

    o Check GST configuration: Gateway of Tally > F11: Features > Statutory & Taxation.
    o Ensure correct GSTIN entries and tax rates.

2. **Reconcile GST Reports:**

    o Navigate to Gateway of Tally > Display > Statutory Reports > GST Reports.
    o Regularly reconcile GSTR-1, GSTR-2A, and GSTR-3B to catch and correct discrepancies.

4. Login Issues

Symptoms:

*   Inability to log in to Tally

Solutions:

1. **Check User Credentials:**

    o Verify username and password are correct.
    o Reset passwords if necessary.

2. **License Activation:**

    o Ensure the Tally license is active: Gateway of Tally > F12: Configure > Licensing.
    o Reactivate or renew the license if expired.

3. **Network Connectivity:**

    o For multi-user environments, ensure network stability.
    o Check server status and connectivity.

5. Voucher Entry Errors

Symptoms:

- Incorrect or missing vouchers

Solutions:

1. **Review Voucher Configurations:**

   - Ensure voucher types are configured correctly: Gateway of Tally > Accounts Info > Voucher Types.

2. **Audit Vouchers:**

   - Use Tally's audit features: Gateway of Tally > Audit & Compliance > Audit Vouchers.
   - Track changes and rectify errors promptly.

6. Printing Issues

Symptoms:

- Incorrect or incomplete printouts

Solutions:

1. **Printer Configuration:**

   - Check printer settings in Tally: Gateway of Tally > F12: Configure > Printing.
   - Ensure the correct printer is selected and configured.

2. **Page Layout and Margins**:

    o   Adjust page layout and margins to fit the document.
    o   Use Tally's Print Preview feature to verify before printing.

7. Backup and Restore Issues

Symptoms:

*   Inability to create or restore backups

Solutions:

1. **Backup Path**:

    o   Ensure the backup path is correctly set: Gateway of Tally > Alt+F3 > Backup.
    o   Verify sufficient disk space is available.

2. **Restore Process**:

    o   Follow the correct restore procedure: Gateway of Tally > Alt+F3 > Restore.
    o   Select the correct backup file and destination.

By understanding and addressing these common issues, you can maintain the smooth operation of Tally and ensure data integrity. Regular maintenance, proper configuration, and timely troubleshooting are key to preventing disruptions. This section provides you with the knowledge to tackle common problems effectively, ensuring a more efficient and reliable Tally experience.

8.2 Best Practices for Accounting

Implementing best practices in accounting can significantly enhance the accuracy, efficiency, and reliability of your financial processes. This chapter outlines key best practices tailored for Tally users, focusing on data management, security, and routine checks. By adopting these practices, you can ensure the integrity of your financial data and streamline your accounting operations.

1. Regular Data Backups

Importance:

- Protects against data loss due to hardware failures, software issues, or other unforeseen events.

Best Practices:

1. **Schedule Regular Backups:**

   o Automate daily or weekly backups depending on the volume of transactions.

   o Navigate to Gateway of Tally > Alt+F3 > Backup to set up backup schedules.

2. **Store Backups in Multiple Locations:**

   o Maintain copies on external drives and cloud storage for added security.

3. **Test Backup Restorations:**

   o Periodically test restoring data from backups to ensure they are functional and up-to-date.

2. Data Security

Importance:

- Ensures sensitive financial information is protected against unauthorized access.

Best Practices:

1. **Implement Strong Passwords:**

   o Use complex passwords for Tally user accounts.
   o Regularly update passwords and avoid sharing them.

2. **User Access Controls:**

   o Set up appropriate user roles and permissions: Gateway of Tally > Alt+F3 > Security Controls.
   o Limit access to sensitive data based on job roles.

3. **Enable Audit Trails:**

   o Track changes and identify unauthorized modifications: Gateway of Tally > Audit & Compliance.

3. Periodic Data Splitting

Importance:

- Maintains optimal performance by reducing the load on Tally's database.

Best Practices:

1. **Split Company Data Periodically**:

   o   At the end of each financial year or when the data volume becomes too large, split the data: Gateway of Tally > Alt+F3 > Split Company Data.

2. **Archive Old Data**:

   o   Move older data to an archive to keep the active database lightweight.

4. Regular Reconciliation

Importance:

- Ensures accuracy in financial records by matching Tally data with external statements.

Best Practices:

1. **Bank Reconciliation**:

   o   Monthly reconcile bank statements with ledger entries: Gateway of Tally > Banking > Bank Reconciliation.

2. **GST Reconciliation**:

   o   Regularly reconcile GSTR-1, GSTR-2A, and GSTR-3B reports to ensure GST accuracy: Gateway of Tally > Display > Statutory Reports > GST Reports.

3. **Vendor and Customer Reconciliation**:

   o Regularly reconcile vendor and customer accounts to ensure accurate outstanding balances.

5. Stay Updated

Importance:

- Ensures compliance with the latest regulatory requirements and leverages new features.

Best Practices:

1. **Software Updates**:

   o Keep Tally updated to the latest version to benefit from new features and security patches: Gateway of Tally > F12: Configure > General > Automatic Updates.

2. **Regulatory Changes**:

   o Stay informed about changes in tax laws and accounting standards.
   o Adjust Tally configurations as necessary to comply with new regulations.

6. Training and Support

Importance:

- Enhances the efficiency and expertise of your accounting team.

Best Practices:

1. **Regular Training**:

    o   Provide ongoing training for your team on Tally features and updates.
    o   Use Tally's built-in help features and online resources for training materials.

2. **Utilize Support Resources**:

    o   Take advantage of Tally's customer support and community forums for troubleshooting and advice.
    o   Participate in Tally webinars and workshops to stay current with best practices and updates.

Adopting these best practices can greatly improve the efficiency, accuracy, and security of your accounting operations in Tally. Regular backups, data security measures, periodic data management, and staying updated with software and regulatory changes are critical for maintaining a robust accounting system. By ensuring your team is well-trained and utilizing available support resources, you can maximize the benefits of Tally and enhance your overall financial management processes.

8.3   Resources and Support

To maximize the benefits of Tally and ensure efficient and effective use, it is essential to leverage the available resources and support systems. This section outlines the various resources provided by Tally, as well as external support options, to help you address issues, stay updated, and continuously improve your accounting processes.

Official Tally Resources

1. Tally Help and Documentation

Importance:

- Provides comprehensive information and step-by-step guides on using Tally features.

Resources:

1. **TallyHelp:**

   - Access Tally's official help documentation via Gateway of Tally > Help or visit TallyHelp.
   - Find detailed articles, FAQs, and how-to guides covering all aspects of Tally.

2. **In-Built Help:**

   - Utilize context-sensitive help within Tally by pressing Alt+H or Ctrl+H while navigating different features.

2. Tally Knowledge Base

Importance:

- Offers a repository of articles and tutorials for troubleshooting and learning advanced features.

Resources:

1. **Knowledge Base:**

   o   Visit the Tally Knowledge Base at Tally Knowledge Base for a wide range of articles on common issues, tips, and tricks.

2. **Case Studies:**

   o   Explore case studies and success stories to learn how other businesses effectively use Tally.

3. Tally Academy and Training

Importance:

-   Provides structured learning opportunities for mastering Tally.

Resources:

1. **Tally Academy:**

   o   Enroll in courses and certification programs offered by Tally Academy to enhance your skills. Visit Tally Academy for more information.

2. **Webinars and Workshops:**

   o   Participate in live webinars and workshops conducted by Tally experts to stay updated on new features and best practices.

External Support and Community

1. Tally Partners and Service Providers

Importance:

- Access professional services for implementation, customization, and troubleshooting.

Resources:

1. **Tally Partners**:

   - Connect with authorized Tally Partners for implementation, customization, and support services. Find a partner near you through the Tally website.

2. **Consultants**:

   - Hire Tally consultants for specialized needs, including data migration, integration with other systems, and advanced training.

2. Online Communities and Forums

Importance:

- Engage with other Tally users to share knowledge, ask questions, and find solutions.

Resources:

1. **Tally Community Forum**:

   - Join the Tally Community Forum at Tally Community to ask questions, share insights, and get help from other Tally users and experts.

2. **Social Media Groups**:

    o   Participate in Tally-related groups on social media platforms like LinkedIn and Facebook for peer support and networking.

Technical Support

1. Tally Customer Support

Importance:

*   Receive direct assistance from Tally's support team for technical issues and queries.

Resources:

1. **Support Portal**:

    o   Access the Tally Support Portal at Tally Support Portal to submit support tickets, track issue resolutions, and find self-help articles.

2. **Contact Support**:

    o   Reach out to Tally customer support via email or phone for direct assistance. Contact details are available on the Tally website.

2. Remote Access Support

Importance:

*   Get real-time assistance for resolving complex issues.

Resources:

1. **Remote Support:**

   o   Tally offers remote support where a support representative can access your system (with permission) to diagnose and fix issues. Schedule a session through the Tally Support Portal.

<u>Conclusion</u>

Utilizing the wide array of resources and support options available for Tally can greatly enhance your experience and ensure you make the most out of the software. From official documentation and training to community support and professional services, these resources are designed to help you troubleshoot issues, stay informed, and continuously improve your accounting practices. Leveraging these tools effectively can lead to more efficient operations and better financial management.

"Every challenge in accounting is an opportunity to refine your skills. By mastering troubleshooting and best practices, you turn obstacles into stepping stones toward efficiency."

CHAPTER 9

Case Studies and Success Stories

Real-world examples of how businesses have successfully implemented and leveraged Tally can provide valuable insights and inspiration for optimizing your own accounting processes. This chapter presents a collection of case studies and success stories, showcasing diverse industries and scenarios where Tally has made a significant impact. By exploring these examples, you'll gain a deeper understanding of best practices, innovative solutions, and the tangible benefits that Tally can bring to your business operations.

9.1 Success Stories from Tally Users

In this chapter, we delve into the real-world impact of Tally software through the lens of various users who have successfully leveraged its features. These success stories highlight how Tally has transformed accounting practices across different sectors, showcasing its versatility and effectiveness. By exploring these cases, we aim to illustrate the tangible benefits of Tally and inspire readers to apply similar strategies in their own businesses.

Case Study 1: Streamlining Small Business Accounting

Background: Meet Rajesh, the owner of a small retail business struggling with the inefficiencies of manual accounting. Rajesh's business faced frequent errors in financial records, lengthy reconciliation processes, and difficulty in generating accurate reports.

Challenges: The manual system led to discrepancies in financial data, delays in reporting, and significant time spent on bookkeeping tasks. Rajesh needed a solution to automate and streamline his accounting processes.

Solution: Rajesh decided to implement Tally, taking advantage of its automated calculations, real-time reporting, and inventory management features. Tally's user-friendly interface and customizable options allowed Rajesh to tailor the software to his specific needs.

Results: The transition to Tally resulted in a dramatic reduction in processing time and errors. Rajesh reported a

50% decrease in time spent on bookkeeping and a significant improvement in financial accuracy. The automated reports enabled better decision-making and provided insights into sales trends and inventory levels, contributing to a 20% increase in profitability.

Case Study 2: Enhancing Financial Management for a Growing Enterprise

Background: Priya, CFO of a mid-sized manufacturing company, faced challenges as her company expanded. Managing multiple branches and consolidating financial data became increasingly complex.

Challenges: Priya's team struggled with integrating financial data from different locations, ensuring compliance with regulatory requirements, and generating consolidated financial reports.

Solution: Priya implemented Tally's multi-location support and advanced reporting features. Tally's centralized database allowed seamless integration of financial data from various branches. Additionally, Tally's compliance features helped ensure adherence to regulatory standards.

Results: The company experienced enhanced financial oversight and streamlined operations. Consolidated reports were generated effortlessly, providing Priya with a clear view of the company's financial health. The improved financial management contributed to a 15% reduction in operational costs and more informed strategic planning.

Case Study 3: Transforming Accounting Practices in a Non-Profit Organization

Background: The Hope Foundation, a non-profit organization, struggled with managing donor funds and generating transparent financial reports for stakeholders.

Challenges: The foundation faced difficulties in tracking donations, managing restricted funds, and providing clear financial statements to donors and regulatory bodies.

Solution: Tally's fund management and donor tracking features were implemented to address these challenges. The software facilitated accurate tracking of donations, management of restricted funds, and generation of detailed financial statements.

Results: The Hope Foundation saw improved transparency in its financial reporting, leading to stronger donor relationships and increased trust. The ability to provide clear and detailed reports resulted in a 25% increase in donations and better compliance with reporting requirements.

Lessons Learned from the above case studies

From these success stories, several key lessons emerge:

- **Proper Implementation**: Effective use of Tally requires careful implementation and customization to fit specific business needs.
- **Training and Support**: Adequate training for users is essential to fully leverage Tally's features and ensure a smooth transition.

- **Utilizing Features**: Taking full advantage of Tally's diverse features, such as automated reporting and multi-location support, can lead to significant improvements in efficiency and accuracy.

The success stories in this chapter demonstrate Tally's ability to address various accounting challenges across different sectors. By automating processes, enhancing financial oversight, and improving transparency, Tally has proven to be a valuable tool for businesses and organizations of all sizes. Readers are encouraged to consider how they might apply similar strategies to unlock the full potential of Tally in their own accounting practices.

9.2 Lessons Learned

In this section, we distill the critical lessons derived from the success stories of Tally users discussed previously. These insights are intended to guide readers in maximizing the effectiveness of Tally software in their own accounting practices. By understanding these lessons, users can avoid common pitfalls, enhance their implementation strategies, and fully leverage Tally's capabilities.

<u>Lesson 1: Proper Implementation is Crucial</u>

The foundation of a successful Tally implementation lies in careful planning and execution. Each business has unique requirements, and a one-size-fits-all approach may not yield the best results.

- **Customize to Fit Needs**: Tailor Tally's features to align with specific business needs. For example, configure modules for inventory management, payroll, or multi-location operations based on your requirements.

- **Initial Setup**: Ensure accurate data migration from existing systems to Tally. This includes setting up the chart of accounts, inventory items, and other relevant data.
- **Integration**: Consider how Tally will integrate with other systems in use, such as CRM or ERP systems, to ensure seamless data flow and functionality.

Best Practices:

- Conduct a thorough needs assessment before implementation.
- Work with Tally consultants or experts to configure the software correctly.
- Perform comprehensive testing before going live to identify and address any issues.

<u>Lesson 2: Training and Support Are Essential</u>

Effective use of Tally requires proper training and ongoing support. Users must be proficient in using the software to realize its full potential.

- **Training Programs**: Provide training sessions for all users to familiarize them with Tally's features and functionalities. Tailor training to different user roles, such as accountants, managers, or administrators.
- **Documentation**: Make use of Tally's documentation and online resources. Encourage users to refer to these materials for self-help and troubleshooting.

- **Ongoing Support**: Establish a support system for users to seek assistance when needed. This could include internal support teams, Tally support services, or community forums.

Best Practices:

- Invest in comprehensive training programs for all users.
- Create user manuals or quick-reference guides specific to your organization's setup.
- Ensure access to ongoing support and updates.

Lesson 3: Utilizing Tally's Features Effectively

Tally offers a wide range of features designed to enhance accounting efficiency. Fully utilizing these features can lead to significant improvements in financial management.

- **Automated Reporting**: Take advantage of Tally's automated reporting features to generate financial statements, tax reports, and other key documents quickly and accurately.
- **Advanced Modules**: Explore and implement advanced modules, such as multi-location support, payroll management, and inventory control, based on your business needs.
- **Customization**: Use Tally's customization options to create reports, forms, and layouts that suit your specific requirements.

Best Practices:

- Regularly review and update your Tally setup to ensure you are utilizing the latest features.

- Customize reports and forms to meet specific business needs and regulatory requirements.
- Explore Tally's add-ons and integrations to enhance functionality.

Lesson 4: Data Accuracy and Security

Ensuring the accuracy and security of financial data is paramount. Tally provides tools to manage and safeguard data, but proper practices must be followed.

- **Data Entry**: Implement controls to minimize errors in data entry, such as validation rules and reconciliation processes.
- **Backup and Recovery**: Regularly back up your Tally data to protect against loss or corruption. Ensure you have a recovery plan in place in case of data issues.
- **Access Controls**: Use Tally's access control features to restrict user access based on roles and responsibilities, ensuring that sensitive data is only accessible to authorized personnel.

Best Practices:

- Establish protocols for accurate data entry and verification.
- Schedule regular backups and test recovery procedures.
- Configure access controls to protect sensitive financial information.

Lesson 5: Continuous Improvement and Adaptation

Explanation: The accounting landscape is constantly evolving, and businesses must adapt to changes to stay competitive. Tally's flexibility allows for continuous improvement and adaptation.

- **Regular Updates**: Stay informed about new features, updates, and enhancements to Tally. Implement updates promptly to take advantage of new functionalities.
- **Feedback Loop**: Encourage feedback from users to identify areas for improvement and address any issues that arise.
- **Adaptation**: Be prepared to adjust your Tally setup and practices as your business grows or changes.

Best Practices:

- Keep up with Tally's updates and new releases.
- Collect and act on feedback from users to improve the system.
- Review and revise your Tally setup periodically to ensure it remains aligned with your business needs.

The lessons learned from Tally users emphasize the importance of proper implementation, effective training, full utilization of features, data accuracy, and continuous improvement. By applying these insights, businesses can optimize their use of Tally, enhance their accounting practices, and achieve greater efficiency and accuracy in financial management.

9.3 Applying Insights to Your Business

In this section, we focus on translating the insights and lessons from Tally success stories into actionable strategies for your own business. Understanding how to apply these insights can help you optimize Tally's use, improve your accounting processes, and drive better financial outcomes.

1. Assessing Your Current Accounting Practices

Before implementing changes, it's crucial to evaluate your existing accounting practices and identify areas for improvement. This assessment helps you understand how Tally can address your specific needs.

- **Review Existing Processes**: Analyze your current accounting methods, including data entry, reporting, and compliance procedures. Identify any inefficiencies, inaccuracies, or bottlenecks.
- **Identify Pain Points**: Determine the key challenges you face, such as manual errors, slow reporting, or difficulties in tracking financial data.
- **Set Objectives**: Define clear objectives for what you want to achieve with Tally, such as increased efficiency, improved accuracy, or better financial insights.

Best Practices:

- Conduct a thorough audit of your current accounting practices.
- Involve key stakeholders in the assessment process.
- Set measurable goals for improvements.

2. Customizing Tally to Meet Your Needs

Tailoring Tally to fit your business requirements ensures that you get the most out of its features and functionalities.

- **Configure Modules**: Customize Tally's modules to align with your specific business needs. For example, set up inventory management for retail businesses or payroll processing for companies with employees.

- **Create Custom Reports**: Use Tally's customization options to design reports that meet your specific requirements. This might include financial statements, tax reports, or management reports.
- **Integrate with Other Systems**: If you use other software for CRM, ERP, or other functions, ensure that Tally integrates seamlessly with these systems for smooth data flow.

Best Practices:

- Work with Tally consultants or experts if needed to customize the software effectively.
- Regularly review and update configurations as your business evolves.
- Test customizations thoroughly before full implementation.

3. Training and Engaging Your Team

Ensuring that your team is well-trained and engaged with Tally is critical for maximizing its benefits.

- **Develop a Training Plan**: Create a training plan that includes initial training sessions for all users, as well as ongoing support and refresher courses.
- **Provide Resources**: Offer access to user manuals, online resources, and support channels to help users troubleshoot issues and learn new features.

- **Encourage Feedback**: Create a feedback loop where users can share their experiences, challenges, and suggestions for improvement.

Best Practices:

- Schedule regular training sessions and updates for your team.
- Monitor user engagement and provide additional support as needed.
- Act on feedback to continuously improve the user experience.

4. Ensuring Data Accuracy and Security

Maintaining data accuracy and security is essential for reliable financial management and compliance.

- **Implement Data Entry Controls**: Use Tally's validation features to minimize errors in data entry. Set up review processes to ensure data accuracy.
- **Establish Backup Procedures**: Regularly back up your Tally data to prevent loss. Implement a recovery plan to address potential data issues.
- **Configure Access Controls**: Set up user roles and permissions to restrict access to sensitive financial information based on job responsibilities.

Best Practices:

- Develop and enforce data entry and verification procedures.
- Schedule regular data backups and test recovery methods.
- Use Tally's security features to protect financial data.

5. Monitoring and Adapting to Changes

The business environment is dynamic, and your accounting practices should adapt to changes to stay relevant and effective.

- **Track Performance**: Use Tally's reporting features to monitor key performance indicators (KPIs) and assess the effectiveness of your accounting processes.
- **Review and Adjust**: Periodically review your Tally setup and accounting practices to ensure they continue to meet your business needs. Make adjustments as necessary.
- **Stay Updated**: Keep abreast of Tally's updates and new features. Implement changes to take advantage of improvements and enhancements.

Best Practices:

- Regularly analyze performance data and adjust practices accordingly.
- Schedule periodic reviews of your Tally setup and processes.
- Stay informed about software updates and incorporate relevant changes.

Conclusion

Applying the insights from Tally success stories to your own business involves assessing current practices, customizing Tally to fit your needs, training and engaging your team, ensuring data accuracy and security, and staying adaptable to changes. By following these strategies, you can optimize Tally's use, enhance your accounting processes, and achieve better financial management outcomes.

"Behind every success story is a lesson in persistence, innovation, and smart decision-making. Case studies offer a blueprint for turning challenges into triumphs."

CHAPTER 10

Conclusion and Next Steps

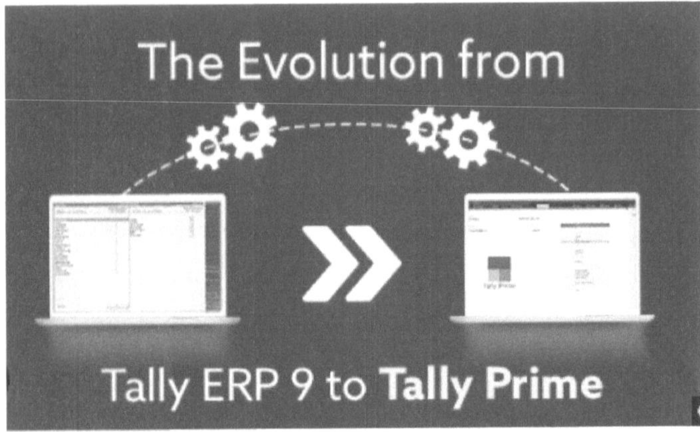

As we reach the end of this journey through optimizing Tally for effective accounting, it's important to reflect on the key takeaways and plan for future progress. This chapter will summarize the core insights gained, highlight the benefits of implementing the strategies discussed, and outline actionable steps to continue enhancing your accounting practices. Embracing these next steps will help you maintain efficiency, adapt to evolving needs, and leverage Tally's full potential for ongoing success.

10.1   Recap of Key Learnings

In this section, we will revisit the fundamental insights and lessons covered throughout the book. This recap aims to consolidate your understanding of how to maximize Tally's capabilities and apply effective accounting practices to drive better business outcomes.

1. Understanding Tally's Core Features

A thorough understanding of Tally's core features is essential for leveraging its full potential. Key features include automated reporting, inventory management, payroll processing, and multi-location support.

- **Automated Reporting**: Tally's ability to generate accurate, timely financial reports reduces manual effort and improves decision-making.
- **Inventory Management**: Efficient tracking of inventory levels, movements, and valuations helps optimize stock management and reduce carrying costs.
- **Payroll Processing**: Streamlined payroll management ensures accurate salary calculations, tax deductions, and compliance with labor laws.
- **Multi-Location Support**: Consolidating financial data from multiple branches or locations simplifies oversight and reporting.

Summary: Mastering these features enables businesses to automate processes, enhance accuracy, and gain valuable insights.

2. Importance of Proper Implementation

Effective implementation is critical to ensuring that Tally meets your specific business needs and integrates seamlessly into your existing processes.

- **Customization**: Tailoring Tally's modules and features to fit your business requirements ensures that you get the most relevant functionality.
- **Integration**: Proper integration with other systems (e.g., CRM, ERP) facilitates smooth data flow and reduces duplication of effort.

Summary: Investing time and effort in the initial setup and customization of Tally sets the foundation for successful usage and long-term benefits.

3. Training and Support for Effective Use

Adequate training and support are crucial for ensuring that all users can effectively utilize Tally's features and functionalities.

- **Training Programs**: Providing comprehensive training helps users understand how to navigate and use Tally effectively.
- **Support Systems**: Ongoing support and access to resources assist users in troubleshooting issues and staying updated with new features.

Summary: Continuous education and support enhance user proficiency and maximize the software's value.

4. Ensuring Data Accuracy and Security

Maintaining data integrity and security is vital for reliable financial management and compliance.

- **Data Entry Controls**: Implementing validation rules and review processes minimizes errors and ensures accurate financial records.
- **Backup and Recovery**: Regular backups and a solid recovery plan protect against data loss and corruption.
- **Access Controls**: Configuring user roles and permissions safeguards sensitive financial information.

Summary: Prioritizing data accuracy and security helps maintain trustworthy financial records and protects against potential risks.

5. Adapting to Changes and Continuous Improvement

The ability to adapt and continuously improve is key to staying competitive and effective in accounting practices.

- **Monitoring Performance**: Regularly reviewing performance metrics and financial data helps identify areas for improvement.
- **Staying Updated**: Keeping up with Tally updates and new features ensures that you benefit from the latest advancements.
- **Feedback and Adaptation**: Soliciting feedback from users and making necessary adjustments fosters a culture of continuous improvement.

Summary: Embracing a mindset of adaptation and improvement ensures that your accounting practices evolve in line with business needs and technological advancements.

This recap reinforces the essential lessons and insights from the book, providing a clear overview of how to leverage Tally for effective accounting. By understanding Tally's features, implementing the software correctly, investing in training, ensuring data accuracy, and remaining adaptable, you can enhance your accounting practices and achieve greater financial success.

10.2   Planning for Future Growth

Effective planning for future growth is crucial for ensuring that your accounting practices and Tally implementation continue to support your business objectives as you scale. This section focuses on strategies for preparing for growth, adapting your Tally setup to evolving needs, and ensuring that your accounting practices remain robust and flexible.

1. Assessing Growth Potential

Before planning for future growth, it's important to evaluate your current growth potential and identify areas that will require attention.

- **Growth Projections**: Analyze your business's growth trajectory, including potential increases in revenue, market expansion, or new product lines.
- **Resource Requirements**: Identify additional resources needed to support growth, such as staff, technology, or infrastructure.
- **Risk Assessment**: Evaluate potential risks associated with growth, including financial, operational, or market-related challenges.

Best Practices:

- Develop a growth forecast and set realistic milestones.
- Plan for scalability in resources and infrastructure.
- Conduct a risk analysis and create mitigation strategies.

2. Scaling Your Tally Implementation

As your business grows, your Tally setup may need to be adjusted to accommodate increased complexity and scale.

- **Upgrading Modules**: Review and upgrade Tally's modules to handle increased transactions, expanded inventory, or additional branches.
- **Enhancing Features**: Utilize advanced Tally features such as multi-location support, consolidated reporting, and customized dashboards to manage larger volumes of data.
- **Integration with Other Systems**: Ensure that Tally integrates effectively with other systems, such as ERP or CRM, to support expanded operations.

Best Practices:

- Regularly review and adjust Tally configurations to match your growth needs.
- Explore additional Tally features or third-party integrations that support scalability.
- Plan for system upgrades or enhancements in advance of expected growth.

3. Optimizing Processes for Efficiency

Streamlining accounting processes is essential for maintaining efficiency as your business grows.

- **Automating Tasks**: Implement automation for repetitive tasks, such as data entry, reporting, and reconciliation, to reduce manual effort and minimize errors.
- **Standardizing Procedures**: Develop standardized procedures and workflows to ensure consistency and efficiency across different departments or locations.
- **Monitoring Performance**: Regularly track key performance indicators (KPIs) to assess the efficiency of your accounting processes and identify areas for improvement.

Best Practices:

- Leverage Tally's automation capabilities to streamline routine tasks.
- Document and standardize accounting procedures for consistency.
- Use performance metrics to evaluate and refine processes.

4. Training and Development for a Growing Team

As your team expands, ensuring that all members are well-trained and aligned with your accounting practices is vital.

- **On boarding New Employees**: Develop a structured on boarding program for new hires, including training on Tally and accounting procedures.
- **Ongoing Education**: Provide continuous learning opportunities to keep your team updated on new features, best practices, and industry trends.

- **Knowledge Sharing**: Foster a culture of knowledge sharing and collaboration to enhance team capabilities and expertise.

Best Practices:

- Create comprehensive on boarding and training programs for new team members.
- Invest in ongoing professional development and certification opportunities.
- Encourage knowledge sharing and best practice discussions within your team.

5. Planning for Technological Advancements

Technology is constantly evolving, and staying ahead of advancements can provide a competitive edge.

- **Monitoring Trends**: Keep abreast of technological trends and innovations in accounting and software solutions.
- **Adopting New Technologies**: Evaluate and adopt new technologies that can enhance your accounting practices, such as AI-driven analytics, cloud-based solutions, or advanced data security measures.
- **Updating Systems**: Regularly update your Tally system and other technology solutions to leverage new features and improvements.

Best Practices:

- Stay informed about industry trends and technological advancements.
- Assess the impact of new technologies on your accounting practices.

- Plan for technology upgrades and transitions to ensure compatibility and effectiveness.

6. Building a Long-Term Strategy

Developing a long-term strategy for growth helps ensure that your accounting practices and Tally implementation align with your overall business objectives.

- **Strategic Planning**: Align your Tally implementation and accounting practices with your long-term business goals and strategic vision.
- **Scalability Planning**: Develop a scalable strategy that accommodates future growth, including infrastructure, resources, and process improvements.
- **Regular Review**: Periodically review and adjust your strategy based on changes in business goals, market conditions, and technological advancements.

Best Practices:

- Create a strategic plan that integrates accounting practices with business objectives.
- Regularly assess and adjust your growth strategy as needed.
- Engage key stakeholders in the strategic planning process to ensure alignment and support.

Planning for future growth involves assessing growth potential, scaling your Tally implementation, optimizing processes, training your team, and staying ahead of technological advancements. By implementing these strategies, you can ensure that your accounting practices remain effective and scalable as your business evolves, ultimately supporting sustained success and growth.

10.3   Continuing Your Education

In the ever-evolving field of accounting and financial management, continuous education is crucial for staying updated with the latest developments, technologies, and best practices. This section explores the importance of ongoing learning, identifies various resources for professional growth, and provides strategies for integrating continuous education into your career and business practices.

1. The Importance of Ongoing Learning

Continuous education is vital for maintaining expertise in accounting and adapting to industry changes. It helps professionals stay competitive, make informed decisions, and leverage new technologies effectively.

- **Industry Evolution**: Accounting standards, regulations, and technologies are constantly evolving. Staying informed ensures you are compliant with current standards and practices.
- **Skill Enhancement**: Ongoing learning allows you to develop new skills and refine existing ones, enhancing your professional capabilities and career prospects.
- **Competitive Edge**: Keeping up with industry trends and advancements gives you a competitive advantage, enabling you to implement innovative solutions and practices.

Best Practices:

- Embrace a mindset of lifelong learning and curiosity.
- Recognize the value of staying current with industry developments.
- Prioritize education as a key component of career growth.

2. Educational Resources and Opportunities

There are numerous resources available for continuing education in accounting, ranging from formal courses to self-directed learning options. Exploring these resources can help you stay informed and enhance your skills.

- **Formal Education**: Consider enrolling in advanced courses, certifications, or degree programs related to accounting, finance, or business management. Institutions and professional bodies often offer specialized programs.
- **Online Courses and Webinars**: Leverage online platforms that provide courses, webinars, and workshops on various accounting topics and Tally software updates.
- **Industry Conferences and Seminars**: Attend industry conferences, seminars, and workshops to network with professionals, gain insights from experts, and learn about the latest trends and technologies.
- **Professional Journals and Publications**: Regularly read industry journals, magazines, and publications to stay updated on new research, practices, and case studies.

Best Practices:

- Research and select reputable educational programs and resources.
- Balance formal education with practical, hands-on learning opportunities.
- Engage with industry professionals and thought leaders through conferences and seminars.

3. Setting Personal and Professional Learning Goals

Establishing clear learning goals helps you focus your efforts and measure your progress in acquiring new knowledge and skills.

- **Identify Areas for Improvement**: Assess your current skills and knowledge to determine areas where you need further education or development.
- **Set Specific Goals**: Define specific, measurable, achievable, relevant, and time-bound (SMART) goals for your learning journey. For example, you might aim to complete a certification within six months or attend two industry conferences annually.
- **Create a Learning Plan**: Develop a structured plan outlining the steps you will take to achieve your learning goals, including selecting courses, allocating time for study, and tracking progress.

Best Practices:

- Regularly review and adjust your learning goals based on your evolving needs and interests.
- Break down larger goals into smaller, manageable milestones.

- Monitor your progress and celebrate achievements along the way.

4. Applying New Knowledge and Skills

Applying what you learn to your daily work and business practices is essential for translating educational experiences into tangible benefits.

- **Implement Best Practices**: Apply new techniques, tools, or methods learned through education to improve your accounting processes and efficiency.
- **Share Knowledge**: Share insights and knowledge with colleagues or team members to foster a culture of continuous improvement within your organization.
- **Evaluate Impact**: Assess the impact of newly acquired skills or knowledge on your work performance and business outcomes. Make adjustments as needed to optimize benefits.

Best Practices:

- Integrate new learnings into your workflow and processes.
- Collaborate with others to implement best practices and drive innovation.
- Regularly evaluate and refine your application of new knowledge to ensure effectiveness.

5. Staying Engaged with Professional Communities

Engaging with professional communities provides opportunities for networking, learning, and staying informed about industry developments.

- **Join Professional Organizations**: Become a member of relevant professional organizations and associations to access resources, attend events, and connect with peers.
- **Participate in Online Forums and Groups**: Engage in online forums, discussion groups, and social media platforms related to accounting and Tally to exchange ideas and seek advice.
- **Seek Mentorship**: Find a mentor or advisor who can provide guidance, support, and insights based on their experience and expertise.

Best Practices:

- Actively participate in professional communities and events.
- Build and maintain relationships with industry peers and mentors.
- Contribute to discussions and share your experiences to benefit others.

Conclusion

Continuing your education is essential for staying current in the accounting field, enhancing your skills, and adapting to industry changes. By leveraging educational resources, setting clear learning goals, applying new knowledge, and engaging with professional communities, you can ensure ongoing growth and success in your career. Embrace the journey of lifelong learning to remain effective, innovative, and competitive in the ever-evolving landscape of accounting and financial management.

"Learning is a lifelong journey. In the ever-evolving world of accounting, continuous education is the key to staying ahead, adapting to change, and driving innovation."

"Lets Learn & Grow together"